Readings in Literary Criticism 18

CRITICS ON HENRY JAMES

Readings in Literary Criticism

CRITICS ON
HENRY JAMES

Readings in Literary Criticism
Edited by J. Don Vann

University of Miami Press
Coral Gables, Florida

CONTENTS

ACKNOWLEDGMENTS

Richard P. Blackmur: from *The Lion and the Honeycomb*. Copyright 1951 by Richard P. Blackmur. Reprinted by permission of Harcourt Brace Jovanovich, Inc.

Van Wyck Brooks: from *The Pilgrimage of Henry James*. Copyright 1925 by E. P. Dutton and Co., Inc.; 1952 by Van Wyck Brooks. Reprinted by permission of the publisher.

Richard Chase: from *The American Novel and Its Traditions*. Copyright © 1957 by Richard Chase. Reprinted by permission of Doubleday and Co.

Leon Edel: from *Henry James: The Untried Years*. Copyright © 1953 by J. B. Lippincott, Inc. Reprinted by permission of the publisher.

Harold C. Goddard: from *Nineteenth Century Fiction,* Vol. 12, no. 1, 1957. Copyright © 1957 by The Regents of the University of California. Reprinted by permission of The Regents.

Percy Lubbock: from *The Craft of Fiction*. Copyright © 1921 by Percy Lubbock. Reprinted by permission of The Viking Press, Inc.

F. O. Matthiessen: from *Henry James: The Major Phase*. Copyright 1944 by Oxford University Press, Inc. Reprinted by permission of the publisher.

Ezra Pound: from *The Literary Essays of Ezra Pound*. Copyright 1918, 1920, 1935 by Ezra Pound. Reprinted by permission of New Directions Publishing Corporation.

Allen Tate: from Commentary on "The Beast in the Jungle" in *The House of Fiction* by Caroline Gordon and Allen Tate. Copyright 1950, © 1960 by Charles Scribner's Sons. Reprinted by permission of the publisher.

Lionel Trilling: from *The Liberal Imagination*. Copyright © 1950 by The Macmillan Company. Reprinted by permission of the publisher.

Dorothy Van Ghent: from *The English Novel*. Copyright © 1953 by Holt, Rinehart and Winston. Reprinted by permission of the publisher.

Edith Wharton: from *A Backward Glance*. Copyright © 1934 by Appleton-Century, Inc. Reprinted by permission of the publisher.

Yvor Winters: from *In Defense of Reason*. Copyright © 1947 by Yvor Winters. Reprinted by permission of The Swallow Press, Chicago.

INTRODUCTION

HENRY JAMES enjoyed the amazing good fortune of an enthusiastic review of his first book by a leading American critic in one of the country's most prominent literary magazines—William Dean Howells in *The Atlantic.* Some contemporary critics did find fault with the novelist. A. M. Logan, for example, saw James's work as failing to represent common experience, and Mrs. Hill rejected the presentation of the British dialogue. (Her review is the only one that James is known to have answered. He, in fact, shunned press notices of his work. See his letter to her in Leon Edel, ed., *Selected Letters of Henry James,* 1960, pp. 69-75.)

In 1905 Elisabeth Cary published the first book-length comprehensive analysis of James's novels. She dwelled in particular on his portrayal of national character and of the moral dilemmas in character development, thus pointing the direction for many subsequent studies. The commentaries by T. S. Eliot, Ezra Pound, and Edith Wharton provide the special insights of artists making observations on the works of a fellow artist.

Van Wyck Brooks in *The Pilgrimage of Henry James* represents those critics who emphasized the alienation theme of American literature, the study of the man without a country. By clarifying the matter of the "obscure hurt" Leon Edel seems to have put an end to much speculation and to have invalidated many studies based on James's supposed impotence. Edel's findings in the five-volume biography display the need for constant reassessment of literary criticism and biography as new materials come to light.

North Texas State University, 1971   J. DON VANN

TABLE OF IMPORTANT DATES

1843	April 15. Henry James born in New York.
1855-1858	In accordance with the theory of Henry James, Sr., that his sons were to be citizens of the world, the family lived at Geneva, London, Paris, and Boulogne.
1858	The family moved to Newport, R. I.
1859	Returned to Geneva.
1860	Moved to Bonn early in the year.
1860	Moved back to Newport.
1862	James goes to Harvard Law School.
1866	The James family established itself in Cambridge, which James came to regard as his American home.
1865-1869	Wrote criticism for *The Nation*.
1869	To Europe.
1871	"A Passionate Pilgrim" published in *The Atlantic*.
1870-1872	In Cambridge.
1875	Having spent the two previous years in Europe and returned to America, James decided that he belonged in Europe.
1876	Settled in London as a permanent residence.
1876	*Roderick Hudson.*
1877	*The American.*
1878	*The Europeans* and *French Poets and Novelists*.
1879	*Daisy Miller, An International Episode, The Madonna of the Future and Other Tales*, and *Hawthorne*.
1881-1883	The American trips.
1881	*The Portrait of a Lady* and *Washington Square*.
1882	James's mother died on Jan. 29; his father on Dec. 18.
1883	*The Siege of London* and *Portraits of Places*.
1884	*Tales of Three Cities.*
1885	*The Author of Beltraffio, Stories Revived*, and *A Little Tour of France*.
1886	*The Bostonians* and *The Princess Casamassima*.
1888	*The Aspern Papers* and *Partial Portraits*.
1889	*A London Life.*
1892	*The Lesson of the Master.*
1893	*The Real Thing and Other Tales, The Private Life, The Wheel of Time, Picture and Text*, and *Essays in London and Elsewhere*.
1894-1895	Contributed stories to *The Yellow Book*.
1894-1895	*Theatricals.*
1895	*Termination.*
1895	Play, *Guy Domville*, produced in London. The hostility of the audience on opening night caused James to abandon his early theatrical aspirations.
1896	*Embarrassments.*
1897	*The Spoils of Poynton* and *What Maisie Knew*.
1898	*The Two Magics* and *In the Cage*.
1899	*The Awkward Age.*

1900	*The Soft Side.*
1901	*The Sacred Fount.*
1902	*The Wings of the Dove.*
1903	*The Better Sort, The Ambassadors,* and *William Wetmore Story and His Friends.*
1904	*The Golden Bowl.*
1904	Traveled in America.
1905-1907	Revised his novels and tales for a collected edition.
1907	*The American Scene.*
1908	Having a renewed interest in the stage, James produced another play, *The High Bid.*
1909	*The Altar of the Dead* and *Italian Hours.*
1910	*The Finer Grain.* Returned to America with his brother William, who died there.
1911	Received honorary degree from Harvard.
1912	Received honorary degree from Oxford.
1913	*A Small Boy and Others.*
1914	*Notes of a Son and Brother.*
1915	Became a British citizen to protest America's isolationism.
1916	February 28. Death of Henry James.
1917	*The Ivory Tower, The Sense of the Past,* and *The Middle Years*—fragments published posthumously.

WILLIAM DEAN HOWELLS

Review of *The Passionate Pilgrim*

MR. HENRY JAMES, JR., has so long been a writer of magazine stories, that most readers will realize with surprise the fact that he now presents them for the first time in book form. He has already made his public. Since his earliest appearance in The Atlantic people have strongly liked and disliked his writing; but those who know his stories, whether they like them or not, have constantly increased in number, and it has therefore been a winning game with him. He has not had to struggle with indifference, that subtlest enemy of literary reputations. The strongly characteristic qualities of his work, and its instantly recognizable traits, made it at once a question for every one whether it was an offense or a pleasure. To ourselves it has been a very great pleasure, the highest pleasure that a new, decided, and earnest talent can give; and we have no complaint against this collection of stories graver than that it does not offer the author's whole range. We have read them all again and again, and they remain to us a marvel of delightful workmanship. In richness of expression and splendor of literary performance, we may compare him with the greatest, and find none greater than he; as a piece of mere diction, for example, The Romance of Certain Old Clothes in this volume is unsurpassed. No writer has a style more distinctly his own than Mr. James, and few have the abundance and felicity of his vocabulary; the precision with which he fits the word to the thought is exquisite; his phrase is generous and ample. Something of an old-time stateliness distinguishes his style, and in a certain weight of manner he is like the writers of an age when literature was a far politer thing than it is now. In a reverent ideal of work, too, he is to be rated with the first. His aim is high; he respects his material; he is full of his theme; the latter day sins of flippancy, slovenliness, and insincerity are immeasurably far from him.

In the present volume we have one class of his romances or novelettes: those in which American character is modified or interpreted by the conditions of European life, and the contact with European personages. Not all the stories of this sort that Mr. James has written are included in this book, and one of the stories admitted—The Romance of Certain Old Clothes—belongs rather to another group, to the more strictly romantic tales, of which the author has printed several in these pages; the scene is in America, and in this also it differs from its present neighbors. There is otherwise uncommon unity in the volume, though it has at first glance that desultory air which no collection of short stories can escape. The same purpose of contrast and suggestion runs through A Passionate Pilgrim, Eugene Pickering, The Madonna of the Future, and

Madame de Mauves, and they have all the same point of view. The American who has known Europe much can never again see his country with the single eye of his old ante-European days. For good or for evil, the light of the Old World is always on her face; and his fellow-countrymen have their shadows cast by it. This is inevitable; there may be an advantage in it, but if there is none, it is still inevitable. It may make a man think better or worse of America; it may be refinement or it may be anxiety; there may be no compensation in it for the loss of that tranquil indifference to Europe which untraveled Americans feel, or it may be the very mood in which an American may best understand his fellow-Americans. More and more, in any case, it pervades our literature, and it seems to us the mood in which Mr. James's work, more than that of any other American, is done. His attitude is not that of a mere admirer of Europe and condemner of America—our best suffers no disparagement in his stories; you perceive simply that he is most contented when he is able to confront his people with situations impossible here, and you fancy in him a mistrust of such mechanism as the cis-Atlantic world can offer the romancer.

However this may be, his book is well worth the carefullest study any of our critics can give it. The tales are all freshly and vigorously conceived, and each is very striking in a very different way, while undoubtedly A Passionate Pilgrim is the best of all. In this Mr. James has seized upon what seems a very common motive, in a hero with a claim to an English estate, but the character of the hero idealized the situation: the sordid illusion of the ordinary American heir to English property becomes in him a poetic passion, and we are made to feel an instant tenderness for the gentle visionary who fancies himself to have been misborn in our hurried, eager world, but who owes to his American birth the very rapture he feels in gray England. The character is painted with the finest sense of its charm and its deficiency, and the story that grows out of it is very touching. Our readers will remember how, in the company of the supposed narrator, Clement Searle goes down from London to the lovely old country-place to which he has relinquished all notion of pretending, but which he fondly longs to see; and they will never have forgotten the tragedy of his reception and expulsion by his English cousin. The proprietary Searle stands for that intense English sense of property which the mere dream of the American has unpardonably outraged, and which in his case wrecks itself in an atrocious piece of savagery. He is imagined with an extraordinary sort of vividness which leaves the redness of his complexion like a stain on the memory; and yet we believe we realize better the dullish kindness, the timid sweetness of the not-at-once handsome sister who falls in love with the poor American cousin. The atmosphere of the story, which is at first that of a novel, changes to the finer air of romance during the scenes at Lockley Park, and you gladly accede to all the romantic conditions, for the sake of otherwise unattainable effects. It is good and true that Searle should not be shocked out of his unrequited affection for England by his cousin's brutality, but should die at Oxford, as he does, in ardent loyalty to his ideal; and it is one of the fortunate inspirations of the tale to confront him there with that decayed and reprobate Englishman in whom abides a longing for the New World as hopeless and unfounded as his own passion for the Old. The character of Miss Searle is drawn with peculiar sweetness and firmness; there is a strange charm in the generous devotion masked by her trepidations and proprieties, and the desired poignant touch is given when at the end she comes only in time to stand by Searle's death-bed. Throughout the story there are great breadths of deliciously sympathetic description. At Oxford the author lights his page with all the rich and mellow picturesqueness of the ancient university town, but we do not know that he is happier there than in his sketches of Lockley Park and Hampton Court, or his study of the old London inn. Everywhere he conveys to you the rapture of his own seeing; one reads such a passage as this with the keen transport that the author felt in looking on the scene itself:—

"The little village of Hampton Court stands clustered about the broad entrance of Bushey Park. After we had dined we lounged along into the hazy vista of the great avenue of horse-chestnuts. There is a rare emotion, familiar to every intelligent traveler, in which the mind, with a great, passionate throb, achieves a magical synthesis of its impressions. You feel England; you feel Italy. The reflection for the moment has an extraordinary poignancy. I had known it from time to time in Italy, and had opened my soul to it as to the spirit of the Lord. Since my arrival in England I had been waiting for it to come. A bottle of excellent Burgundy at dinner had perhaps unlocked to it the gates of sense; it came now with a conquering tread. Just the scene around me was the England of my visions. Over against us, amid the deep-hued bloom of its ordered gardens, the dark red palace, with its formal copings and its vacant windows, seemed to tell of a proud and splendid past; the little village nestling between park and palace, around a patch of turfy common, with its tavern of gentility, its ivy-towered church, its parsonage, retained to my modernized fancy the lurking semblance of a feudal hamlet. It was in this dark, composite light that I had read all English prose; it was this mild, moist air that had blown from the verses of English poets; beneath these broad acres of rain-deepened greenness a thousand honored dead lay buried."

A strain of humor which so pleasantly characterizes the descriptions of the London inn tinges more sarcastically the admirable portrait of the shabby Rawson at Oxford, and also colors this likeness of a tramp—a fellow-man who has not had his picture better done:—

"As we sat, there came trudging along the road an individual whom from afar I recognized as a member of the genus 'tramp.' I had read of the British tramp, but I had never yet encountered him, and I brought my historic consciousness to bear upon the present specimen. As he approached us he slackened pace and finally halted, touching his cap. He was a man of middle age, clad in a greasy bonnet, with greasy earlocks depending from its sides. Round his neck was a grimy red scarf, tucked into his waistcoat; his coat and trousers had a remote affinity with those of a reduced hostler. In one hand he had a stick; on his arm he bore a tattered basket, with a handful of withered green stuff in the bottom. His face was pale, haggard, and degraded beyond description, a singular mixture of brutality and finesse. He had a history. From what height had he fallen, from what depth had he risen? Never was a form of rascally beggarhood more complete. There was a merciless fixedness of outline about him, which filled me with a kind of awe. I felt as if I were in the presence of a personage—an artist in vagrancy.

" 'For God's sake, gentlemen,' he said, in that raucous tone of weather-beaten poverty suggestive of chronic sore throat exacerbated by perpetual gin,—'for God's sake, gentlemen, have pity on a poor ferncollector!'—turning up his stale dandelions. 'Food hasn't passed my lips, gentlemen, in the last three days.'

"We gaped responsive, in the precious pity of guileless Yankeeism. 'I wonder,' thought I, 'if half a crown would be enough?' And our fasting botanist went limping away through the park with a mystery of satirical gratitude superadded to his general mystery."

Mr. James does not often suffer his sense of the ludicrous to relax the sometimes over-serious industry of his analysis, and when he has once done so, he seems to repent it. Yet we are sure that the poetic value of A Passionate Pilgrim is enhanced by the unwonted interfusion of humor, albeit the humor is apt to be a little too scornful. The tale is in high degree imaginative, and its fascination grows upon you in the reading and the retrospect, exquisitely contenting you with it as a new, fine, and beautiful invention.

In imaginative strength it surpasses the other principal story of the book. In Madame de Mauves the spring of the whole action is the idea of an American girl who will have none but a French nobleman for her husband. It is not a vulgar adoration of rank in her, but a young girl's belief that ancient lineage, circumstances of the highest civilization, and opportunities of the greatest refinement, must result in the noblest type of character. Grant the premises, and the effect of her emergence into the cruel daylight of facts is unquestionably tremendous: M. le Baron de Mauves is frankly unfaithful to his American wife, and, finding her too dismal in her despair, advises her to take a lover. A difficulty with so French a situation is that only a French writer can carry due conviction of it to the reader. M. de Mauves, indeed, justifies himself to the reader's sense of likelihood with great consistency, and he is an extremely suggestive conjecture. Of course, he utterly misconceives his wife's character and that of all her race, and perceives little and understands nothing not of his own tradition:

"They talked for a while about various things, and M. de Mauves gave a humorous account of his visit to America. His tone was not soothing to Longmore's excited sensibilities. He seemed to consider the country a gigantic joke, and his urbanity only went so far as to admit that it was not a bad one. Longmore was not, by habit, an aggressive apologist for our institutions; but the baron's narrative confirmed his worst impressions of French superficiality. He had understood nothing, he had felt nothing, he had learned nothing; and our hero, glancing askance at his aristocratic profile, declared that if the chief merit of a long pedigree was to leave one so vaingloriously stupid, he thanked his stars that the Longmores had emerged from obscurity in the present century, in the person of an enterprising lumber merchant. M. de Mauves dwelt of course on that prime oddity of ours, the liberty allowed to young girls; and

related the history of his researches into the 'opportunities' it presented to
French noblemen, researches in which, during a fortnight's stay, he seemed to
have spent many agreeable hours. 'I am bound to admit,' he said, 'that in every
case I was disarmed by the extreme candor of the young lady, and that they
took care of themselves to better purpose than I have seen some mammas in
France take care of them.' Longmore greeted this handsome concession with
the grimmest of smiles, and damned his impertinent patronage."

This is all very good character, and here is something from the baron that
is delicious:

"I remember that, not long after our marriage, Madame de Mauves undertook to read me one day a certain Wordsworth, a poet highly esteemed, it
appears, *chez vous*. It seemed to me that she took me by the nape of the neck
and forced my head for half an hour over a basin of *soupe aux choux,* and that
one ought to ventilate the drawing-room before any one called."

The baron's sister, in her candid promotion of an intrigue between Madame
de Mauves and Longmore, we cannot quite account for even by the fact that
she hated them both. But Madame de Mauves is the strength of the story, and
if Mr. James has not always painted the kind of women that women like to
meet in fiction, he has richly atoned in her lovely nature for all default. She
is the finally successful expression of an ideal of woman which has always been
a homage, perhaps not to all kinds of women, but certainly to the sex. We
are thinking of the heroine of Poor Richard, of Miss Guest in Guest's Confession, of Gabrielle de Bergerac in the story of that name, and other gravely sweet
girls of this author's imagining. Madame de Mauves is of the same race, and
she is the finest,—as truly American as she is womanly; and in a peculiar
fragrance of character, in her purity, her courage, her inflexible high-minded-
ness, wholly of our civilization and almost of our climate, so different are her
virtues from the virtues of the women of any other nation.

The Madonna of the Future is almost as perfect a piece of work, in its way,
as A Passionate Pilgrim. It is a more romantic conception than Madame de
Mauves, and yet more real. Like A Passionate Pilgrim, it distinguishes itself
among Mr. James's stories as something that not only arrests the curiosity, stirs
the fancy, and interests the artistic sense, but deeply touches the heart. It is
more than usually relieved, too, by the author's humorous recognition of the
pathetic absurdity of poor Theobald, and there is something unusually good
in the patience with which the handsome, common-minded Italian woman of
his twenty years' adoration is set before us. Our pity that his life should have
slipped away from him in devout study of this vulgar beauty, and that she
should grow old and he should die before he has made a line to celebrate her
perfection or seize his ideal, is vastly heightened by the author's rigid justice
to her; she is not caricatured by a light or a shadow, and her dim sense of
Theobald's goodness and purity is even flattered into prominence. In all
essentials one has from this story the solid satisfaction given by work in which
the conception is fine, and the expression nowhere falls below it—if we except
one point that seems to us rather essential, in a thing so carefully tempered
and closely wrought. The reiteration of the Italian figure-maker's philosophy,

"Cats and monkeys, monkeys and cats; all human life is there," is apparently of but wandering purport, and to end the pensive strain of the romance with it is to strike a jarring note that leaves the reader's mind out of tune. Sometimes even the ladies and gentlemen of Mr. James's stories are allowed a certain excess or violence in which the end to be achieved is not distinctly discernible, or the effect so reluctantly responds to the intention as to leave merely the sense of the excess.

Eugene Pickering is, like Madame de Mauves, one of those realistic subjects which we find less real than the author's romantic inspirations. There is no fault with the treatment; that is thoroughly admirable, full of spirit, wit, and strength; but there is a fancifulness in the outlines of Pickering's history and the fact of his strange betrothal which seems to belong to an old-fashioned stage-play method of fiction rather than to such a modern affair as that between the unsophisticated American and Madame Blumenthal; it did not need that machinery to produce this effect, thanks to common conditions of ours that often enough keep young men as guileless as Pickering, and as fit for sacrifice at such shrines as hers. However, something must always be granted to the story-teller by way of premises; if we exacted from Mr. James only that he should make his premises fascinating, we should have nothing to ask here. His start, in fact, is always superb; he possesses himself of your interest at once, and he never relinquishes it till the end; though there he may sometimes leave your curiosity not quite satisfied on points such as a story-teller assumes to make it clear. What, for example, were exactly the tortuous workings of Madame Blumenthal's mind in her self-contradictory behavior towards Pickering? These things must be at least unmistakably suggested.

Since Hawthorne's Donatello, any attempt to touch what seems to be the remaining paganism in Italian character must accuse itself a little, but The Last of the Valeri is a study of this sort that need really have nothing on its conscience. It is an eminently poetic conceit, though it appeals to a lighter sort of emotions than any other story in Mr. James's book; it is an airy fabric woven from those bewitching glimpses of the impossible which life in Italy affords, and which those who have enjoyed them are perfectly right to overvalue. It has just the right tint of ideal trouble in it which no living writer could have imparted more skillfully than it is here done. If the story is of slighter material than the others, the subtlety of its texture gives it a surpassing charm, and makes it worthy to be named along with the only other purely romantic tale in the book.

To our thinking, Mr. James has been conspicuously fortunate in placing his Romance of Certain Old Clothes in that eighteenth-century New England when the country, still colonial, was no longer rigidly puritanic, and when a love of splendor and accumulating wealth had created social conditions very different from those conventionally attributed to New England. It is among such bravely dressing provincials as Copley used to paint, and as dwelt in fine town mansions in Boston, or the handsome country-places which still remember their faded grandeur along Brattle Street in Cambridge, that Mr. James finds the circumstance and material of his personages; and we greatly enjoy the novelty of this conception of what not only might, but must have existed hereabouts in times which we are too prone to fancy all close-cropped and sad-colored. The tale is written with heat, and rapidly advances from point to point, with a constantly mounting interest. The sisterly rivalry is shown with due boldness, but without excess, and the character of Viola is sketched with vigor that conveys a full sense of her selfish, luxurious beauty. The scene between her and Perdita when the engagement of the latter is betrayed, the scene in which she unrolls the stuff of the wedding-dress and confronts herself in the glass with it falling from her shoulder, and that in which she hastily tries the garment on after her sister's marriage, are pictures as full of character as they are of color. The most is made of Perdita where she lies dying, and bids her husband keep her fine clothes for her little girl; it is very affecting indeed, and all the more so for the explicit human-nature of the dying wife's foreboding. In the whole course of the story nothing is urged, nothing is dwelt upon; and all our story-tellers, including Mr. James himself, could profitably take a lesson from it in this respect. At other times he has a tendency to expatiate upon his characters too much, and not to trust his reader's perception enough. For the sake of a more dramatic presentation of his persons, he has told most of the stories in this book as things falling within the notice of the assumed narrator; an excellent device; though it would be better if the assumed narrator were able to keep himself from seeming to patronize the simpler-hearted heroes, and from openly rising above them in a worldly way.

But this is a very little matter, and none of our discontents with Mr. James bear any comparison to the pleasure we have had in here renewing our acquaintance with stories as distinctly characteristic as anything in literature. It is indeed a marvelous first book in which the author can invite his critic to the same sort of reflection that criticism bestows upon the claims of the great reputations; but one cannot dismiss this volume with less and not slight it. Like it or not, you must own that here is something positive, original, individual, the result of long and studious effort in a well-considered line, and mounting in its own way to great achievement. We have a reproachful sense of leaving the immense suggestiveness of the book scarcely touched, and we must ask the reader to supply our default from the stories themselves. He may be assured that nothing more novel in our literature has yet fallen in his way; and we are certain that he will not close the book without a lively sense of its force. We can promise him also his own perplexities about it, among which may be a whimsical doubt whether Mr. James has not too habitually addressed himself less to men and women in their mere humanity, than to a certain kind of cultivated people, who, well as they are in some ways, and indispensable as their appreciation is, are often a little narrow in their sympathies and poverty-stricken in the simple emotions; who are so, or try to be so, which is quite as bad, or worse.

From "Recent Fiction," *The Atlantic,* 35 (April 1875), 490-95.

MRS. F. H. HILL

Review of *Daisy Miller*

IT IS right in all ways that Mr. Henry James's last two volumes, "Daisy Miller and Other Stories" (Macmillan and Co.), should take their title from the first and principal story. It is not an "important" work in the sense in which picture-dealers use the word. It is not long, being told in 193 not closely-printed pages; it is not pretentious, it has very little plot, not much of a beginning, and no end at all. But it is rare work. If we were not all so extremely tired of "word-painting," both of the name and the thing itself, we should call this work of Mr. James's a perfect specimen of a minute word-picture. Let no one imagine we are classing it with the sort of description which was introduced some years ago by an able hand, and has since been copied and recopied, and washed over and chromo-lithographed, so to speak *ad nauseam*. That style, especially if written throughout in the present tense, a practice which helps much to facility of production, bad grammar, easy writing, and hard reading, is not at all difficult, and not at all uncommon. Work such as "Daisy Miller" is very uncommon. It has no air of difficulty about it, nor the least effect of labour or strain. Yet scarcely one of Palmaroli's dainty beauties has been more carefully studied in her conscious fashionable prettiness than Daisy Miller in her innocent fashionable simplicity. So well depicted is she, so cleverly has every accessory been put in around her, so cunningly has she been placed in just the right distance for survey, that she becomes a real personage, and, though we do not remember whether her voice is anywhere spoken of or described, we are quite certain that we know what her voice was like, and in what delicate modulation she uttered her little Americanisms. The group of persons surrounding this bright pathetic little figure is drawn with singular clearness, humour, and happy lightness of touch. The scapegrace of a brother; the ineffective Mrs. Miller; the subtle Italian who knew his world too well ever to harbour a suspicion of Daisy's innocence in his not otherwise particularly trustful mind; the cautious Winterbourne, whose density poor Daisy could not penetrate with a sweet voice or bright eyes, are all admirably done. In these, as in his other books, it is noticeable that Mr. James is courageous with his Americans. The best and most refined of them use words and phrases which other English-speaking persons are accustomed to think vulgar. The eternal beginning of every sentence "Well," the "I guess," and "I shouldn't think you'd want to," the use of "real" in the sense of "very" (and by the way, it would seem from some observation of American poetry that "real" is pronounced in America as if it were written "reel"), the "going round" and "getting through" (in the sense in which a gentleman is asked if he will soon "be through" his dinner), sound oddly coming from the lips of ladies and gentlemen. The courage is the courage of sympathy and liking, it would appear; for the odd phrases do not seem vulgar when Mr. James's people use them— they seem only quaint. This grace, however, of drawing vulgar people who are not vulgar, our author chooses, as he has a perfect right to do, to restrict to his own countrymen and women. When he has to deal with English people, his cunning or his will is laid aside. We feel bound to protest against the manners of Lord Lambeth and Mr. Percy Beaumont, in "An International Episode," being received as typical of the manners of English gentlemen. As individual characters we take them on their merits and judge them accordingly, but true as types they certainly are not. There are undoubtedly, in England, and out of it, plenty of 'Arries, 'Arries in all grades of society, 'Arries even going about with the dread title "lord." Had Mr. James chosen to draw for our amusement an 'Arry, he would have done it with all his wonted humour and truth, and greatly amused we should have been. But Lord Lambeth and Percy Beaumont are not 'Arries. They are very worthy, stupid, honest gentlemen, and acquit themselves consistently as such in all they do. Why then should they be represented as habitually talking like arrant 'Arries? Men who have presumably been to a public school and college do not preface all their remarks with "Oh, I say!" That is not the slang of the stable or the club. That is the slang of the street, and Mr. James does not choose his English titles happily, nor are the manners of his English fine ladies pretty. Perhaps he does not consider that English manners are pretty, and we have no doubt he has had ample means of judging. We have left ourselves no space to dwell on the third and last of these "Stories," and in effect it is not a story. It is a study, an episode, an interlude, not a sketch, because the lines are bitten in with too great depth and intensity. It is a sad etching. It has been translated into French, and published in the "Revue des Deux Mondes" under the name of "Les Quatre Rencontres." No one who reads it will fail to see how the little tale recommended itself to the French mind, and how well it is adapted for a French dress. It might be a wonderfully clever translation of a French story, by Charles de Bernard; or even, to pay Mr. James a higher compliment, it might be an English rendering from Turguenieff.

From "Recent Novels," *The Daily News* (London), 21 March 1879, p. 6.

H. E. SCUDDER

Review of *The Tragic Muse*

MR. JAMES has achieved a kind of success in his latest novel which goes far to illustrate a great canon of the art of fiction. The mind of his readers may be taken to reflect his mind, and we make the assertion with confidence that if, after reading the novel as it has been appearing in The Atlantic, with delight in the brilliancy of the group of portraits which it presents, they now take up the two comely volumes in which the serial is gathered, their attention will be held by what may be called the spiritual plot of the tale. That which first commands admiration may not have been first in the author's mind, but it was first in the order of presentation. The artistic defect in novels of a purpose is that the function of the novel as a reproduction of life is blurred by the function of the tract. On the other hand, the artistic defect in the novel without a purpose lies in a superficial dexterity which supposes life itself to be shallow and incapable of anything more than a surface gleam. It is in the nice portrayal of surfaces, by which an undercurrent of moving life is now revealed, now concealed, that the highest art is disclosed. Sometimes this undercurrent is made manifest by the steady movement of the characters toward some final catastrophe; sometimes it is brought to light in the relation of characters to each other as illustrative of a single large theme, and in such cases neither tragedy nor comedy is necessarily resultant; the issue may be in the decision of each person, the definite fixing of the place of each in some microcosm.

It is this latter class of novels, where the judgment of the persons delineated is not emphasized and made unmistakable by a rude confirmation of external circumstance, that is winning the regard of the most thoughtful and most penetrating writers. And is it not characteristic of a view of life at once profound and bright that the creator of fictitious forms should be indifferent to *coups de théâtre,* and should care most for those human judgments which seem best to reflect divine judgment? For the lightning does not strike the blasphemer, vengeance does not fall swiftly upon the parricide, hell does not open before the betrayer of innocence. It is a finer power which discerns the crumbling of the interior defenses of the human citadel, and discloses the ruin by glimpses through the fair exterior. Surely the art of novelist is acquiring a wider range when to the novel of adventure, the novel of dramatic completeness, the novel of character, is added the novel which gives us a picture of human life as it passes before the spectator, who might himself be a part of it, and at the same time offers an interpretation of that life, and attempts something like a generalization of the sub-order to which it belongs.

This, at any rate, is what we conceive Mr. James has done for us in The
Tragic Muse. As we have intimated, after we have admired the brilliancy of
the figures which compose the group constantly before the sight, we become
even more interested in the revelation of those characters to the mind by the
patient and apparently inexhaustible art of the novelist, showing them by the
aid of a few incidents only, but of innumerable expressions in situation and
converse. The simple theme on which Mr. James plays with endless variations
is profound enough to justify all the labor which he has expended in illustrating
it. We are tempted to say, in the light of his great success, that it is the only
adequate mode by which the theme could be treated in fiction. For the relations
of man to art admit of and demand such subtlety of thought that the fine shades
of these relations can only be distinguished by the most painstaking setting
forth of delicate workings of this thought in action and speech. Thus, as one
recalls the wealth of phrase in which this masterly work abounds, he will admit
that it is the lavishness of true art, not the prodigality of a spendthrift in words.
Follow as one will the lines of movement in the novel, they all lead to the
few fundamental, authoritative principles which form the groundwork of the
novel. To the careless reader there is a waste of material in determining the
question whether or not Nick Dormer is to marry Julia, whether Peter Sherringham is to marry Biddy or Miriam. He may be amused by the suspense in
which he is kept, and entertained indefinitely by the spirited dialogue, but,
judging the novel by its issue, he would have his own applause if he demanded,
Is the game worth the candle?

The triumph of the novelist, in our judgment, lies in the fact that he can
hold the careless reader to the close, cajoling him with the notion that he is
in for the matrimonial hunt of the conventional novel, while at the same time
he slowly opens to the student of life a singularly interesting relation of the
progress of human souls, each moving toward its determination by choice and
the gravitation of nature, and presenting constantly fresh examples of the
problems of which they are themselves only now and then distinctly conscious.
Perhaps the subtlest of these disclosures is in the delicately suggested nature
of the attitude which Miriam Rooth holds at the last toward Nick Dormer.
The real stanchness of the artist's fidelity to his art is seen in the sincerity of
his dealings with Julia Dallow, and his absolute immobility under the tentative
advances of Miriam. Indeed, the reader comes to have a sense of compassion
for the tragedienne which is nowhere directly solicited by the author. He reads
between the lines, not because the author has written a story faintly there, but
because he has described the persons so truthfully, so completely, that, given
the persons and situations, this unexpressed relation is inevitable. Here is an
artist brave with no heroics, but through the simple honesty of his nature. He
is the rock toward which Miriam turns, uncompromising in fidelity to her art,
as instanced by her penetrating disclosure of Sherringham's nature, but also
conscious of her own feminine dependency. It was a stroke of genius, and not
the *pis aller* of a novelist intent upon pairing off his characters, which made
her contemptuously tuck Basil Dashwood under her arm at the last.

Mr. James, to the thinking of many, gave himself space enough for the explication of his theme, but it is clear that he limited himself deliberately by recognizing in his study of the relations of art to life only two forms of art, the pictorial and the histrionic. He needed two because he needed both Nick Dormer and Miriam Rooth; and some of his happiest interpretations of the entire theme are in the glimpses which he gives of Nick Dormer's attitude toward portrait-painting. Once, at least, also, he throws in a fine illustration from the art of writing when Gabriel Nash says:

"Life consists of the personal experiments of each of us and the point of an experiment is that it shall succeed. What we contribute is our treatment of the material, our rendering of the text, our style. A sense of the qualities of a style is so rare that many persons should doubtless be forgiven for not being able to read, or at all events to enjoy us. But is that a reason for giving it up, for not being, in this other sphere, if one possibly can, a Macaulay, a Ruskin, a Renan? Ah, we must write our best; it's the great thing we can do in the world, on the right side. One has one's form, *que diable,* and a mighty good thing that one has. I'm not afraid of putting life into mine, without unduly squeezing it. I'm not afraid of putting in honor and courage and charity, without spoiling them; on the contrary, I'll only do them good. People may not read you at sight, may not like you, but there's a chance they'll come round; and the only way to court the chance is to keep it up—always to keep it up. That's what I do, my dear fellow, if you don't think I've perseverance. If some one likes it here and there, if you give a little impression of solidity, that's your reward: besides, of course, the pleasure for yourself."

Nash is a writer, though the fact is lightly stated, and Mr. James has not worked him as a *littérateur*. It is sometimes hard to say just what he meant to make of the figure, whose personality is faintly sketched, and who seems scarcely more than a stalking-horse of clever approaches to the main game; his taking off is the most effective part. The great character of the book is the title character, and the art which is most elaborately analyzed is the histrionic. The actual development of the perfected artist out of the crude shape in which we first discover Miss Rooth is not given. Instead we have the much more interesting study of Miss Rooth in her earlier phase, and then, presto! change! the Miss Rooth who blazes forth. For the author's interest and the reader's is not in how to make a great artist out of unpromising material, but how, when the artist is made, everything looks to her. There are few more deft touches in this clever book than the genuine surprise which all enjoy, Sherringham, Dormer, Madame Carré, and the reader, when the cocoon is broken and the brilliant butterfly emerges.

It is a striking illustration of Mr. James's power of handling his material that from first to last Miriam Rooth is always seen *en face*. That is to say, though their author indulges in analysis of his other characters, he gives the reader only a front view of his heroine. When she appears she is on exhibition. We see her reflected occasionally in the faces of her audience, but we are not helped to a more intimate knowledge through the private advices of her creator. The brilliancy of the effect is greatly enhanced by this means, and the sort of theatrical show which goes on is wonderfully effective as a mode of carrying off the study which Mr. James is constantly making of the tragedian's art, as seen in the attitude toward it of the tragedian himself, or, as in this case, herself. He seems to ask himself, How would a girl having this genius for the stage regard herself, the stage, the play, the critic, the audience; how even would she look upon marriage, so universally regarded as the crown of a woman's life. But inasmuch as this artistic life is led in the glare of publicity, he preserves the illusion by making Miss Rooth ask all these questions, as it were, in public. There are no concealments, and there is no evasion. The persistency with which histrionic art in its personal aspect is pursued, without any wearisome, impersonal discussion, is most admirable. The unfolding of this theme is the unfolding of the story. Not for a moment does the reader find himself in any eddies of conversation; he is always in the current. It would be easy to quote passage after passage in illustration of the wit, the insight, the broad sense, which mark the development of this interior plot of the story, but we should only be printing over again what already has been printed in these pages. We can only advise students of literature and art who wish to see how a fine theme may be presented with a technique which, at first blush, would seem inconsistent with breadth of handling, but on closer scrutiny proves to be the facile instrument of a master workman who is thinking of the soul of his art, to read The Tragic Muse.

From "The Tragic Muse," *The Atlantic,* 66 (1890), 419-22.

A. M. LOGAN

Three Early Reviews

Essays in London and Elsewhere.—The Wheel of Time, and Other Stories.— The Private Life, and Other Stories. Harper & Bros.

IN THE essay on Gustave Flaubert included in Mr. James's volume, 'Essays in London and Elsewhere,' when referring to the few people who understand what Flaubert tried for, the author says, "it is only when a reader is also a writer and a tolerably tormented one that he particularly cares." This is an example of the personal note occasionally struck in the volume, and echoes like a response to the sound of many voices clamoring criticism of Mr. James. No writer of fiction has suffered more from the people who won't or can't understand what he is trying for, while none has more consistently directed his energy towards one issue—the perfection of form and expression. Public obtuseness is probably more real than affected, for there is nothing of which the average Anglo-Saxon has less intuitive appreciation than of literary form apart from subject, except, it may be, of the resources of his own language. One may deplore such defective perception, but can hardly regard it as a valid excuse for angry rejection of every effort at education.

When he publishes a volume of essays, Mr. James gets the better of his more vociferous censors. The subjects are labelled, and, at least, the general drift is obvious. His knowledge and his sympathetic comprehension of his chosen subjects' meaning may be realized by every one, but there still remains enough sensitive penetration to puzzle a resentful multitude. The only essay which can hope for unqualified approval both from the public and from the literary class is that on James Russell Lowell. Mr. Lowell's mind, says Mr. James, had "little affinity with superfine estimates and shades and tints of opinion," and in writing of him Mr. James shakes off his own preoccupation with shades and tints, and takes on much of his subject's freedom, fullness, and warmth. He makes no attempt to classify Mr. Lowell either as author or diplomatist, but he draws a beautiful living portrait of the man at the moment when he stepped from the library into the great world, and he follows with loving yet clear-sighted enthusiasm the development of a career which he characterizes as, in the last analysis, a tribute to the dominion of style. This combination of affectionate sympathy with clearness of vision makes Mr. James's best qualification for criticism. Those with whom he cannot, for one reason or another, sympathize he kindly neglects, and on the other hand his judgment is never impaired by the glow of personal congeniality. He recognizes that his function is to enlighten, and he chooses to do that by emphasizing merits rather than defects.

Cordial approval is his prevailing mood, except when judging 'The Journal of the Brothers de Goncourt,' a performance which invites much harsher terms than Mr. James employs. Though his greatest admiration is reserved for the writers' writers, in his estimate of Mrs. Humphry Ward he is wholly with the public—a rather surprising testimony to catholicity of taste. It is useless to dispute the charm of a book so phenomenally successful as 'Robert Elsmere,' but that charm, for the English public, probably owes more than Mr. James perceives to the purely didactic element. In his remarks on Henrik Ibsen he gives full value to the power of a moral question to agitate the British breast. The few pages devoted to Ibsen are more acute and comprehensive than all the screeds of his English adorers and antagonists put together. One gets away from the endless irrelevant chatter about his morality or immorality, and is permitted calmly to consider him as a dramatist, a man with an almost infallible sense of dramatic effect, quite unscrupulous in the choice of subjects through which the effect is to be wrought. He is not set forth as a Shakespere or a Dante dealing with eternal verities applicable to every era and phase of human life. He is a dramatist of extraordinary intellect and more extraordinary imagination, but with national, local, and even parochial limitations. His magic lies in the wonderful vivification of an assemblage mostly commonplace and vulgar, or abnormally vicious. Mr. James emphasizes Ibsen's lack of humor, and there is a moment when we fear that by temporary infection his own admirable sense of the humorous has been impaired. It is when he supposes Ibsen, in 'Hedda Gabler,' to be "playing with an idea from the simple instinct of sport," and qualifies the play as an "ironical pleasantry." This may be an ingenious explanation of the dreadful Hedda, but it seems to represent the author as too monstrous in his play.

It is perhaps not fair to pass directly from Mr. James's critical work to his fiction. The judgment of practice by principle is too immediate, and the operation may have the air of the cold-blooded attempt to hang a man with a rope of his own spinning. Yet, when two volumes of fiction lie beside the essays, the temptation to consider them in order is irresistible. In the essays the vexed question of subject and form in literature receives much incidental attention. Mr. James naturally leans to the opinion that good form may save a poor subject and that bad form must lose a good subject. He is not quite convinced that the idea is good enough if the expression is, but he thinks the idea is the author's affair and not the critic's. Strict adherence to this principle would almost reduce criticism to comment on technicalities, and would compel it to desist from any estimate of the author's value in literature, literature being considered as a commodity or luxury, with the aesthetic gratification and spiritual elevation of mankind for *raison d'être*. The perfection of the word cannot kill, but, enshrining no perceptible idea, it is an empty and vain thing.

With a clear notion of what Mr. James is trying for, and with thankful recognition of the effort, we get from his two latest volumes of fiction the impression of form without substance, of fine-spun elusive phantoms with no claim on emotional regard, and rather irritating to the intelligence. One has no objection to the fine quality of the garment clothing figures mostly artificial or trivial, but a resentful sense of waste. There are times, too, when the garment fails to please or satisfy, when the phrase is so subtle or so elliptical that lucidity is missed. Such failure is especially noticeable in the conversations, where the reader has often to rely on the descriptive sentence, "he said with a laugh," or "she answered gravely," for a cue to the mental attitude of the characters and an adjustment of his own. Close attachment to refinement of expression is also detracting from Mr. James's creative force. Finish of phrase is not, for instance, characteristic of the British matron, no matter how exalted her station. This somewhat heavy, worldly, and inane personage makes a frequent appearance in these stories, but we cannot think that she ever appeared elsewhere with such polished and vivacious sentences at her tongue's end. It may please Mr. James to toy with this ponderous figure, but the reality recedes from view in proportion to the elaboration of his presentment.

Failure to give the sense of life is of course the irretrievable fault in fiction. We do not mean to burden Mr. James with the imputation of a positive failure in the essential of his art, but only to indicate a possible result from an obvious cause. By the perfection of his rendering of an episode, a situation, a state of the mind or soul, he has achieved unique distinction in English letters; but, to take a place in what he calls the great tradition, his exquisite method must be applied to subjects that are well in the range of common experience, and that appeal with some passion to intelligence and emotion.

From "Henry James," *The Nation,* 57 (1893), 416-17.

ELISABETH CARY

The American

IN READING *Roderick Hudson* to-day it is impossible not to let the mind wander from the book to the reality, so close the book obviously is to the reality, and from the past to the greatly different present; it is during these vagrant moments that one perceives how gently the tone of time has descended upon the pages; they have mellowed and taken on a unity of colour and impression that could not have been recognised in them when they came fresh from the press, the natural effect of age upon the sincere expression of truth in any form of art. What may have seemed a little sharp and thin at the moment it was written is now seen to have conformed to the slightly sharp and thin quality of the scenes and natures described; is seen, too, as the natural note of inexperience, and especially is seen to be the result of the strong sense of responsibility; the instinct of a fine and subtle truthfulness triumphing over a rich imagination in the effort to see life as it is. It was the kind of practice that makes perfect if carried on to the logical end; it was the bondage that makes freedom; it was the attention to truth of substance and truth of manner that makes in time beauty.

In *The American,* that followed *Roderick Hudson* after an interval of two years, the step toward beauty is nothing less than a stride. It carries the author, previously punctilious to the verge of stiffness, into flowery gardens of freedom, a freedom marked by his easier handling of his figures, his lightness of touch in manipulating his greater plot, and above all by his manner of good fellowship with his reader, that manner which was to carry him so far in the mystery of style. Already he stood sufficiently aloof from his own country to see the relation borne by the American to the foreigner. The beautiful study of Christopher Newman is accomplished with great simplicity in the mild, winning manner of the later novels. Uncontentious, delicate, generous in his relation towards others, frankly without superficial taste, but with endless inner refinements of kindness and conscience, Newman stands against the background of family arrogance and tradition among the French nobility, a presentation of his country's quality such as the unfortunate Roderick might have been proud to equal in a sculptured symbol. The charm of Madame de Cintré, martyred in the great French cause of "family," is no less potent and is communicated by the same mild method. The love of form accountable for the inflexibility of Roderick Hudson had already passed into the flowing expression of culture. Culture, Matthew Arnold has determined for us by two rounded definitions, the familiar "knowing the best that has been thought and known in the world" and the less familiar "getting the power through reading to estimate the proportion and relation in what we read." Whether Mr. James got it through reading or through writing, in *The American* a similar power to realise proportion and relation is present in visible and appreciable shape. It is the first purely artistic result of his passion for artistic embodiment of thought. The care for art in it is extreme, and it is somewhat significant that this early writing has so little of the tremulous sensibility in which youth abounds; and that it has so much painstaking, so much groping concern for propriety of expression, so much careful preparation of the matter. It betrays the fact that the preoccupation of its author with form is not an acquired and grafted characteristic. It was at the beginning his strength and his weakness, yet always more his strength than his weakness. It was the latter in fact only so far as it helped to suppress the expression of a poetic perception as rare as it is exquisite. When in the fire of Spring a young talent is cautious, one too insistently remembers that

> The Bird of Time has but a little way
> To flutter and the Bird is on the Wing.

It is not, however, to the purpose to think of how a talent would have been had it been different. It is difficult enough to think truly how in itself it is. In the case of Mr. James caution and responsibility fastening themselves on the shoulders of youth surely sufficiently have justified their grasp. The poetry has found its way out and has been perhaps strengthened and enriched by the husbandry that would not let it push prematurely into sight. Self-consciousness with him has passed into poise, cultivation has brought forth luxuriant bloom. And the fact that he composed from the beginning with his eye "on the object," that he saturated himself from year to year with the experience upon which it was his steady intention to draw for his pictures of life, gave his work the consistent quality of fidelity, the quality that wraps it together. He gave his perceptions that play essential to their growth, recorded the reports they made to him with accurate care, and held himself as disinterestedly as possible in the attitude of a spectator. Full of vitality and curiosity, neither of which apparently has waned in the course of a long service, he curbed his sensibility and the egoism which, since he was young, he must have had, with a remarkable respect for the conditions by which good literature is nourished. If he was "detached," if he did not give himself away in his books as much as Dickens or Thackeray or George Eliot, he was not less of his race and nation for that. To be transparent, effusive, gushing, he says in his article on Daudet "has never been and will never be the ideal of us of English speech," and the dignity of his early style suggests the normal later flowering in the manner of Anglo-Saxon genius.

The American is the novel which we may take as on the whole perhaps most representative of his early quality, and as in its kind a masterpiece of simple rather than complex art, but unmistakably of art. It contains a number of important characters none, in fact, that can be called unimportant, so closely is each fitted into the scheme or plot and made to contribute to the development.

Christopher Newman, however, the "American," entirely dominates the interesting group. To him is owing the profound sense of life in the book. If Mr. James did intend, as by the title we are justified in assuming, to make him the image of his country, the concrete representation of an abstraction, he accomplished his object in a way very different from that pursued by other inventors of our supposed type. For one thing, he absolutely refrained from feeding the vanity of his countrymen by making his American an incarnation of a moral or political or national idea. The democratic spirit of Christopher Newman, if by democratic spirit we mean the pride of liberty to do as one pleases without consulting others, is sufficiently obvious; but it is introduced without the tacit glorification of its virtues common to writers of less subtlety and less breeding. "One's theories, after all, matter little," Newman's creator somewhere says in reference to his method of pursuing culture, "it is one's humour that is the great thing." The American's humour is so much the greatest thing about him that despite his shrewdness, he survives in direct line with Colonel Newcome and the good, dull Dobbin, as one of the gentlest figures in fiction. It was a happy result, the happiest, of an attempt to embody our national characteristic, that, in place of the flamboyant merits on which in literature we have more or less depended for impressiveness, we should see ourselves depicted as possessing the spiritual delicacy ordinarily associated with races of immemorial politeness. Newman has in due degree the idiosyncrasies that make for common recognition of him as an American product. He is a money-maker, who has won his way through difficulties usual enough in the generation of Americans to which he belongs. At the age of fourteen he had been set adrift in the Western world: "necessity had taken him by his slim young shoulders and pushed him into the street to earn that night's supper." It illustrates the choice of adventure commonly made by Mr. James that history begins after the material difficulties are surmounted and the problem has become, how to enjoy the material welfare.

His democracy of enjoyment is a part of his Americanism. Taking his holiday in Paris he likes the great gilded rooms of his showy hotel; he likes driving rapidly and expensively through the country to see the monuments of history; his ideal of giving a "party" for the celebration of his engagement with the lovely Claire de Cintré is to invite every one who has shown him a minimum of politeness and every one with whom he has a shadow of friendship, and to entertain them with singers and actresses of first quality hired at great cost for the charming and intimate occasion. On the other hand his susceptibility to finer impressions is equally marked, and, with a subtlety of suggestion worthy of the cause, this susceptibility is made to appear also a part of Newman's Americanism, a part so integral as to seem the real essence of everything, the element impossible to change without destroying the organism.

"You are the great Western Barbarian," Mrs. Tristram says to him, "stepping forth in his innocence and might, gazing a while at this poor effete Old World, and then swooping down on it." To this indictment Newman replies with remonstrance. "I am a highly civilised man," he contends, "I stick to that. If you don't believe it I should like to prove it to you." The extent to which he proves it is the psychological basis of the story. The extent of his politeness is the touchstone by which the different characters are tested. If the word appears to minify his frank and sturdy temper it can only be because we allow it a superficial meaning alone and decline to trace it to its deep source in consideration for the comfort of others. At all events, it is clearly enough politeness in Newman that gives him his great air of superiority in the presence of the old French noblesse, and that makes his kind simplicity a force in contrast with their complexity of manner. It is the absence of politeness in the complex Bellegarde manner that constitutes its weakness and converts it by insidious shades into absurdity. It is the politeness of Madame de Cintré that makes her a star of charm in the cold constellation of her relatives, before we are aware of her superior moral virtue. It is the grace of politeness in her younger brother Valentin that makes him the true head of the house of Bellegarde. At the end of the story, which takes, its many readers will remember, a melodramatic turn involving criminal acts and startling disclosures, the politeness by which Newman expresses his rich spirit of benignity blossoms into a state of feeling beside which the cheaper states so frequently encountered both in fiction and in life, seem as tawdry as a milliner's display after the blooming summer hedges. The unfortunate American, duped by his French antagonists, but in possession of their hideous secret for revelation or not as he may choose, has been gazing at the gray walls of the convent to which Madame de Cintré had been driven. Turning away, he walked down to the edge of the Seine and saw above him the soft vast towers of Notre Dame.

From *The Novels of Henry James* (New York: G. P. Putnam's Sons, 1905), pp. 58-72.

T. S. ELIOT

The Hawthorne Aspect

In Memory

HENRY JAMES has been dead for some time. The current of English literature was not appreciably altered by his work during his lifetime; and James will probably continue to be regarded as the extraordinarily clever but negligible curiosity. The current hardly matters; it hardly matters that very few people will read James. The "influence" of James hardly matters: to be influenced by a writer is to have a chance inspiration from him; or to take what one wants; or to see things one has overlooked; there will always be a few intelligent people to understand James, and to be understood by a few intelligent people is all the influence a man requires. What matters least of all is his place in such a Lord Mayor's show as Mr. Chesterton's procession of Victorian Literature. The point to be made is that James has an importance which has nothing to do with what came before him or what may happen after him; an importance which has been overlooked on both sides of the Atlantic.

I do not suppose that any one who is not an American can *properly* appreciate James. James's best American figures in the novels, in spite of their trim definite outlines, the economy of strokes, have a fullness of existence and an external ramification of relationship which a European reader might not easily suspect. The Bellegarde family, for instance, are merely good outline sketches by an intelligent foreigner; when more is expected of them, in the latter part of the story, they jerk themselves into only melodramatic violence. In all appearance Tom Tristram is an even slighter sketch. Europeans can recognize him; they have seen him, known him, have even penetrated the Occidental Club; but no European has the Tom Tristram element in his composition, has anything of Tristram from his first visit to the Louvre to his final remark that Paris is the only place where a white man can live. It is the final perfection, the consummation of an American to become, not an Englishman, but a European—something which no born European, no person of any European nationality, can become. Tom is one of the failures, one of nature's misfortunes, in this process. Even General Packard, C. P. Hatch, and Miss Kitty Upjohn have a reality which Claire de Cintré misses. Noémie, of course, is perfect, but Noémie is a result of the intelligent eye; her existence is a triumph of the intelligence, and it does not extend beyond the frame of the picture.

For the English reader, much of James's criticism of America must merely be something taken for granted. English readers can appreciate it for what it has in common with criticism everywhere, with Flaubert in France and Turgenev in Russia. Still, it should have for the English an importance beyond the work of these writers. There is no English equivalent for James, and at least he writes in this language. As a critic, no novelist in our language can approach James; there is not even any large part of the reading public which knows what the word "critic" means. (The usual definition of a critic is a writer who cannot "create"—perhaps a reviewer of books). James was emphatically not a successful *literary* critic. His criticism of books and writers is feeble. In writing of a novelist, he occasionally produces a valuable sentence out of his own experience rather than in judgment of the subject. The rest is charming talk, or gentle commendation. Even in handling men whom he could, one supposes, have carved joint from joint—Emerson, or Norton—his touch is uncertain; there is a desire to be generous, a political motive, an admission (in dealing with American writers) that under the circumstances this was the best possible, or that it has fine qualities. His father was here keener than he. Henry was not a literary critic.

He was a critic who preyed not upon ideas, but upon living beings. It is criticism which is in a very high sense creative. The characters, the best of them, are each a distinct success of creation: Daisy Miller's small brother is one of these. Done in a clean flat drawing, each is extracted out of a reality of its own, substantial enough; everything given is true for that individual; but what is given is chosen with great art for its place in a general scheme. The general scheme is not one character, nor a group of characters in a plot or merely in a crowd. The focus is a situation, a relation, an atmosphere, to which the characters pay tribute, but being allowed to give only what the writer wants. The real hero, in any of James's stories, is a social entity of which men and women are constituents. It is, in *The Europeans,* that particular conjunction of people at the Wentworth house, a situation in which several memorable scenes are merely timeless parts, only occurring necessarily in succession. In this aspect, you can say that James is dramatic; as what Pinero and Mr. Jones used to do for a large public, James does for the intelligent. It is in the chemistry of these subtle substances, these curious precipitates and explosive gases which are suddenly formed by the contact of mind with mind, that James is unequalled. Compared with James's, other novelists' characters seem to be only accidentally in the same book. Naturally, there is something terrible, as disconcerting as quicksand, in this discovery, though it only becomes absolutely dominant in such stories as *The Turn of the Screw.* It is partly foretold in Hawthorne, but James carried it much farther. And it makes the reader, as well as the personae, uneasily the victim of a merciless clairvoyance.

James's critical genius comes out most tellingly in his mastery over, his baffling escape from, Ideas; a mastery and an escape which are perhaps the last test of a superior intelligence. He had a mind so fine that no idea could violate it. Englishmen, with their uncritical admiration (in the present age) for France, like to refer to France as the Home of Ideas; a phrase which, if we could twist it into truth, or at least a compliment, ought to mean that in France ideas are very severly looked after; not allowed to stray, but preserved for the inspection of civic pride in a Jardin des Plantes, and frugally dispatched on occasions of public necessity. England, on the other hand, if it is not the Home of Ideas, has at least become infested with them in about the space of time within which Australia has been overrun by rabbits. In England ideas run wild and pasture on the emotions; instead of thinking with our feelings (a very different thing) we corrupt our feelings with ideas; we produce the political, the emotional idea, evading sensation and thought. George Meredith (the disciple of Carlyle) was fertile in ideas; his epigrams are a facile substitute for observation and inference. Mr. Chesterton's brain swarms with ideas; I see no evidence that it thinks. James in his novels is like the best French critics in maintaining a point of view, a view-point untouched by the parasite idea. He is the most intelligent man of his generation.

The fact of being everywhere a foreigner was probably an assistance to his native wit. Since Byron and Landor, no Englishman appears to have profited much from living abroad. We have had Birmingham seen from Chelsea, but not Chelsea seen (really *seen*) from Baden or Rome. There are advantages, indeed, in coming from a large flat country which no one wants to visit: advantages which both Turgenev and James enjoyed. These advantages have not won them recognition. Europeans have preferred to take their notion of the Russian from Dostoevski and their notion of the American from, let us say, Frank Norris if not O. Henry. Thus, they fail to note that there are many kinds of their fellowcountrymen, and that most of these kinds, similarly to the kinds of their fellow-countrymen, are stupid; likewise with Americans. Americans also have encouraged this fiction of a general type, a formula or idea, usually the predaceous square-jawed or thinlipped. They like to be told that they are a race of commercial buccaneers. It gives them something easily escaped from, moreover, when they wish to reject America. Thus the novels of Frank Norris have succeeded in both countries; though it is curious that the most valuable part of *The Pit* is its satire (quite unconscious I believe; Norris was simply representing faithfully the life he knew) of Chicago society after business hours. All this show of commercialism which Americans like to present to the foreign eye James quietly waves aside; and in pouncing upon his fellow-countryman after the stock exchange has closed, in tracking down his vices and absurdities across the Atlantic, and exposing them in their highest flights of dignity or culture, James may be guilty of what will seem to most Americans scandalously improper behaviour. It is too much to expect them to be grateful. And the British public, had it been more aware, would hardly have been more comfortable confronted with a smile which was so far from breaking into the British laugh. Henry James's death, if it had been more taken note of, should have given considerable relief "on both sides of the Atlantic," and cemented the Anglo-American Entente.

The Hawthorne Aspect

My object is not to discuss critically even one phase or period of James, but merely to provide a note, *Beitrage,* toward any attempt to determine his antecedents, affinities, and "place". Presumed that James's relation to Balzac, to Turgenev, to any one else on the continent is known and measured—I refer to Mr. Hueffer's book and to Mr. Pound's article—and presumed that his relation to the Victorian novel is negligible, it is not concluded that James was simply a clever young man who came to Europe and improved himself, but that the soil of his origin contributed a flavour discriminible after transplantation in his latest fruit. We may even draw the instructive conclusion that this flavour was precisely improved and given its chance, not worked off, by transplantation. If there is this strong native taste, there will probably be some relation to Hawthorne; and if there is any relation to Hawthorne, it will probably help us to analyse the flavour of which I speak.

When we say that James is "American", we must mean that this "flavour" of his, and also more exactly definable qualities, are more or less diffused throughout the vast continent rather than anywhere else; but we cannot mean that this flavour and these qualities have found literary expression throughout the nation, or that they permeate the work of Mr. Frank Norris or Mr. Booth Tarkington. The point is that James is positively a continuator of the New England genius; that there is a New England genius, which has discovered itself only in a very small number of people in the middle of the nineteenth century and which is *not* significantly present in the writings of Miss Sara Orne Jewett, Miss Eliza White, or the Bard of Appledore whose name I forget. I mean whatever we associate with certain purlieus of Boston, with Concord, Salem, and Cambridge, Mass.: notably Emerson, Thoreau, Hawthorne and Lowell. None of these men, with the exception of Hawthorne, is individually very important; they all can, and perhaps ought to be made to look very foolish; but there is a "something" there, a dignity, about Emerson for example, which persists after we have perceived the taint of commonness about some English contemporary, as for instance the more intelligent, better educated, more alert Matthew Arnold. Omitting such men as Bryant and Whittier as absolutely plebeian, we can still perceive this halo of dignity around the men I have named, and also Longfellow, Margaret Fuller and her crew, Bancroft and Motley, the faces of (later) Norton and Child pleasantly shaded by the Harvard elms. One distinguishing mark of this distinguished world was very certainly leisure; and importantly not in all cases a leisure given by money, but insisted upon. There seems no easy reason why Emerson or Thoreau or Hawthorne should have been men of leisure; it seems odd that the New England conscience should have allowed them leisure; yet they *would* have it, sooner or later. That is really one of the finest things about them, and sets a bold frontier between them and a world which will at any price avoid leisure, a world in which Theodore Roosevelt is a patron of the arts. An interesting document, of this latter world is the *Letters* of a nimbly dull poet of a younger generation, of Henry James's generation, Richard Watson Gilder, Civil Service Reform, Tenement House Commission, Municipal Politics.

Of course leisure in a metropolis, with a civilized society (the society of Boston was and is quite uncivilized but refined beyond the point of civilization) with exchange of ideas and critical standards would have been better; but these men could not provide the metropolis, and were right in taking the leisure under possible conditions.

Precisely this leisure, this dignity, this literary aristocracy, this unique character of a society in which the men of letters were also of the best people, clings to Henry James. It is some consciousness of this kinship which makes him so tender and gentle in his appreciations of Emerson, Norton and the beloved Ambassador. With Hawthorne, as much the most important of these people in any question of literary art, his relation is more personal; but no more in the case of Hawthorne than with any of the other figures of the background is there any consideration of influence. James owes little, very little, to anyone; there are certain writers whom he consciously studied, of whom Hawthorne was not one; but in any case his relation to Hawthorne is on another plane from his relation to Balzac, for example. The influence of Balzac, not on the whole a good influence, is perfectly evident in some of the earlier novels; the influence of Turgenev is vaguer, but more useful. That James was, at a certain period, more moved by Balzac, that he followed him with more concentrated admiration, is clear from the tone of his criticism of that writer compared with the tone of his criticism of either Turgenev or Hawthorne. In *French Poets and Novelists*, though an early work, James's attitude toward Balzac is exactly that of having been very much attracted from his orbit, perhaps very wholesomely stimulated at an age when almost any foreign stimulus may be good, and having afterwards reacted from Balzac, though not to the point of injustice. He handles Balzac shrewdly and fairly. From the essay on Turgenev there is on the other hand very little to be got but a touching sense of appreciation; from the essay on Flaubert even less. The charming study of Hawthorne is quite different from any of these. The first conspicuous quality in it is tenderness, the tenderness of a man who had escaped too early from an environment to be warped or thwarted by it, who had escaped so effectually that he could afford the gift of affection. At the same time he places his finger, now and then, very gently, on some of Hawthorne's more serious defects as well as his limitations.

> "The best things come, as a general thing, from the talents that are members of a group; every man works better when he has companions working in the same line, and yielding the stimulus of suggestion, comparison, emulation."

Though when he says that

> "there was manifestly a strain of generous indolence in his (Hawthorne's) composition"

he is understating the fault of laziness for which Hawthorne can chiefly be blamed. But gentleness is needed in criticising Hawthorne, a necessary thing to remember about whom is precisely the difficult fact that the soil which produced him with his essential flavour is the soil which produced, just as inevitably, the environment which stunted him.

In one thing alone Hawthorne is more solid than James: he had a very acute historical sense. His erudition in the small field of American colonial history was extensive, and he made most fortunate use of it. Both men had that sense of the past which is peculiarly American, but in Hawthorne this sense exercised itself in a grip on the past itself; in James it is a sense of the sense. This, however, need not be dwelt upon here. The really vital thing, in finding any personal kinship between Hawthorne and James, is what James touches lightly when he says that

> "the fine thing in Hawthorne is that he cared for the deeper psychology, and that, in his way, he tried to become familiar with it."

There are other points of resemblance, not directly included under this, but this one is of the first importance. It is, in fact, almost enough to ally the two novelists, in comparison with whom almost all others may be accused of either superficiality or aridity. I am not saying that this "deeper psychology" is essential, or that it can always be had without loss of other qualities, or that a novel need be any the less a work of art without it. It is a definition; and it separates the two novelists at once from the English contemporaries of either. Neither Dickens nor Thackeray, certainly, had the smallest notion of the "deeper psychology"; George Eliot had a kind of heavy intellect for it (Tito) but all her genuine feeling went into the visual realism of *Amos Barton*. On the continent it is known; but the method of Stendhal or of Flaubert is quite other. A situation is for Stendhal something deliberately constructed, often an illustration. There is a bleakness about it, vitalised by force rather than feeling, and its presentation is definitely visual. Hawthorne and James have a kind of sense, a receptive medium, which is not of sight. Not that they fail to make you *see,* so far as necessary, but sight is not the essential sense. They perceive by antennae; and the "deeper psychology" is here. The deeper psychology indeed led Hawthorne to some of his absurdest and most characteristic excesses; it was for ever tailing off into the fanciful, even the allegorical, which is a lazy substitute for profundity. The fancifulness is the "strain of generous indolence", the attempt to get the artistic effect by meretricious means. On this side a critic might seize hold of *The Turn of the Screw,* a tale about which I have many doubts; but the actual working out of this is different from Hawthorne's, and we are not interested in approximation of the two men on the side of their weakness. The point is that Hawthorne was acutely sensitive to the situation; that he did grasp character through the relation of two or more persons to each other; and this is what no one else, except James, has done. Furthermore, he does establish, as James establishes, a solid atmosphere, and he does, in his quaint way, get New England, as James gets a larger part of America, and as none of their respective contemporaries get anything above a village or two, or a jungle. Compare, with anything that any English contemporary could do, the situation which Hawthorne sets up in the relation of Dimmesdale and

Chillingworth. Judge Pyncheon and Clifford, Hepzibah and Phoebe, are similarly achieved by their relation to each other; Clifford, for one, being simply the intersection of a relation to three other characters. The only dimension in which Hawthorne could expand was the past, his present being so narrowly barren. It is a great pity, with his remarkable gift of observation, that the present did not offer him more to observe. But he is the one English-writing predecessor of James whose characters are *aware* of each other, the one whose novels were in any deep sense a criticism of even a slight civilization; and here is something more definite and closer than any derivation we can trace from Richardson or Marivaux.

The fact that the sympathy with Hawthorne is most felt in the last of James's novels, *The Sense of the Past,* makes me the more certain of its genuiness. In the meantime, James has been through a much more elaborate development than poor Hawthorne ever knew. Hawthorne, with his very limited culture, was not exposed to any bewildering variety of influences. James, in his astonishing career of self-improvement, touches Hawthorne most evidently at the beginning and end of his course; at the beginning, simply as a young New Englander of letters; at the end, with almost a gesture of approach. *Roderick Hudson* is the novel of a clever and expanding young New Englander; immature, but just coming out to a self-consciousness where Hawthorne never arrived at all. Compared with *Daisy Miller* or *The Europeans* or *The American* its critical spirit is very crude. But *The Marble Faun* (*Transformation*), the only European novel of Hawthorne, is of Cimmerian opacity; the mind of its author was closed to new impressions though with all its Walter Scott-Mysteries of Udolpho upholstery the old man does establish a kind of solid moral atmosphere which the young James does not get. James in *Roderick Hudson* does very little better with Rome than Hawthorne, and as he confesses in the later preface, rather fails with Northampton.[1]

He does in the later edition tone down the absurdities of Roderick's sculpture a little, the pathetic Thirst and the gigantic Adam; Mr. Striker remains a failure, the judgement of a young man consciously humourising, too suggestive of Martin Chuzzlewit. The generic resemblance to Hawthorne is in the occasional heavy facetiousness of the style, the tedious whimsicality how different from the exactitude of *The American Scene,* the verbalism. He too much identifies himself with Rowland, does not see through the solemnity he had created in that character, commits the cardinal sin of failing to "detect" one of his own characters. The failure to create a situation is evident: with Christiana and Mary, each nicely adjusted, but never quite set in relation to each other. The interest of the book for our present purpose is what he does *not* do in the Hawthorne way, in the instinctive attempt to get at something larger, which will bring him to the same success with much besides.

The interest in the "deeper psychology", the observation, and the sense for

1. Was Hawthorne at all in his mind here? In criticising the *House of the Seven Gables* he says "it renders, to an initiated reader, the impression of a summer afternoon in an elm-shaded New England town", and in the preface to *Roderick Hudson* he says "what the early chapters of the book most 'render' to me today is not the umbrageous air of their New England town."

situation, developed from book to book, culminate in *The Sense of the Past* (by no means saying that this is his best) uniting with other qualities both personal and racial. James's greatness is apparent both in his capacity for development as an artist and his capacity for keeping his mind alive to the changes in the world during twenty-five years: It is remarkable (for the mastery of a span of American history) that the man who did the Wentworth family in the '80s could do the Bradhams in the '00s. In *The Sense of the Past* the Midmores belong to the same generation as the Bradhams; Ralph belongs to the same race as the Wentworths, indeed as the Pyncheons. Compare the book with *The House of the Seven Gables* (Hawthorne's best novel after all); the situation, the "shrinkage and extinction of a family" is rather more complex, on the surface, than James's with (so far as the book was done) fewer character relations. But James's real situation here, to which Ralph's mounting the step is the key, as Hepzibah's opening of her shop, is a situation of different states of mind. James's situation is the shrinkage and extinction of an idea. The Pyncheon tragedy is simple; the "curse" upon the family a matter of the simplest fairy mechanics. James has taken Hawthorne's ghost-sense and given it substance. At the same time making the tragedy much more etherial: the tragedy of that "Sense", the hypertrophy, in Ralph, of partial civilization; the vulgar vitality of the Midmores in their financial decay contrasted with the decay of Ralph in his financial prosperity, when they precisely should have been the civilisation he had come to seek. All this watched over by the absent, but conscious Aurora. I do not want to insist upon the Hawthorneness of the confrontation of the portrait, the importance of the opening of a door. We need surely not insist that this book is the most important, most substantial sort of thing that James did; perhaps there is more solid wear even in that other unfinished *Ivory Tower*. But I consider that it was an excursion which we could well permit him, after a lifetime in which he had taken talents similar to Hawthorne's and made them yield far greater returns than poor Hawthorne could harvest from his granite soil; a permissible exercise, in which we may by a legitimately cognate fancy seem to detect Hawthorne coming to a mediumistic existence again, to remind a younger and incredulous generation of what he really was, had he had the opportunity, and to attest his satisfaction that that opportunity had been given to James.

From "In Memory" and "The Hawthorne Aspect," *The Little Review*, 5 (August 1918), 44-53.

EZRA POUND

Henry James

THIS ESSAY on James is a dull grind of an affair, a Baedecker to a continent. I set out to explain, not why Henry James is less read than formerly—I do not know that he is. I tried to set down a few reasons why he ought to be, or at least might be, more read.

Some say that his work was over, well over, finely completed; there is mass of that work, heavy for one man's shoulders to have borne up, labour enough for two lifetimes; still we would have had a few more years of his writing. Perhaps the grasp was relaxing, perhaps we should have had no strongly-planned book; but we should have had paragraphs here and there, and we should have had, at least, conversation, wonderful conversation; even if we did not hear it ourselves, we should have known that it was going on somewhere. The massive head, the slow uplift of the hand, *gli occhi onesti e tardi,* the long sentences piling themselves up in elaborate phrase after phrase, the lightning incision, the pauses, the slightly shaking admonitory gesture with its 'wu-a-wait a little, wait a little, something will come'; blague and benignity and the weight of so many years' careful, incessant labour of minute observation always there to enrich the talk. I had heard it but seldom, yet it is all unforgettable.

The man had this curious power of founding affection in those who had scarcely seen him and even in many who had not, who but knew him at second hand.

No man who has not lived on both sides of the Atlantic can well appraise Henry James; his death marks the end of a period. *The Times* says: 'The Americans will understand his changing his nationality', or something of that sort. The 'Americans' will understand nothing whatsoever about it. They have understood nothing about it. They do not even know what they lost. They have not stopped for eight minutes to consider the meaning of his last public act. After a year of ceaseless labour, of letter writing, of argument, of striving in every way to bring in America on the side of civilization, he died of apoplexy. On the side of civilization—civilization against barbarism, civilization, not Utopia, not a country or countries where the right always prevails in six weeks! After a lifetime spent in trying to make two continents understand each other, in trying, and only his thoughtful readers can have any conception of how he had tried, to make three nations intelligible one to another. I am tired of hearing pettiness talked about Henry James's style. The subject has been discussed enough in all conscience, along with the minor James. Yet I have heard no word of the major James, of the hater of tyranny; book after early book against oppression, against all the sordid petty personal crushing oppression, the domination of modern life; not worked out in the diagrams of Greek tragedy, not labelled 'epos' or 'Aeschylus'. The outbursts in *The Tragic Muse,* the whole of *The Turn of the Screw,* human liberty, personal liberty, the rights of the individual against all sorts of intangible bondage! The passion of it, the continual passion of it in this man who, fools said, didn't 'feel'. I have never yet found a man of emotion against whom idiots didn't raise this cry.

And the great labour, this labour of translation, of making America intelligible, of making it possible for individuals to meet across national borders. I think half the American idiom is recorded in Henry James' writing, and whole decades of American life that otherwise would have been utterly lost, wasted, rotting in the unhermetic jars of bad writing, of inaccurate writing. No English reader will ever know how good are his New York and his New England; no one who does not see his grandmother's friends in the pages of the American books. The whole great assaying and weighing, the research for the significance of nationality, French, English, American.

'An extraordinary old woman, one of the few people who are really doing anything good.' There were the cobwebs about connoisseurship, etc. but what do they matter? Some yokel writes in the village paper, as Henley had written before, 'James's stuff was not worth doing.' Henley has gone pretty completely. America has not yet realized that never in history had one of her great men abandoned his citizenship out of shame. It was the last act—the last thing left. He had worked all his life for the nation and for a year he had laboured for the national honour. No other American was of sufficient importance for his change of allegiance to have constituted an international act; no other American would have been welcome in the same public manner. America passes over these things, but the thoughtful cannot pass over them.

Armageddon, the conflict? I turn to James' *A Bundle of Letters;* a letter from 'Dr Rudolph Staub' in Paris, ending:

> You will, I think, hold me warranted in believing that between precipitate decay and internecine enmities, the English-speaking family is destined to consume itself and that with its decline the prospect of general pervasiveness to which I allude above, will brighten for the deep-lunged children of the fatherland!

We have heard a great deal of this sort of thing since; it sounds very natural. My edition of the volume containing these letters was printed in 1883, and the imaginary letters were written somewhat before that. I do not know that this calls for comment. Henry James' perception came thirty years before Armageddon. That is all I wish to point out. Flaubert said of the War of 1870: 'If they had read my *Education Sentimentale,* this sort of thing wouldn't have happened.' Artists are the antennae of the race, but the bullet-headed many will never learn to trust their great artists. If it is the business of the artist to make humanity aware of itself; here the thing was done, the pages of diagnosis. The multitude of wearisome fools will not learn their right hand from their left or seek out a meaning.

It is always easy for people to object to what they have not tried to understand.

I am not here to write a full volume of detailed criticism, but two things I do claim which I have not seen in reviewers' essays. First, that there was emotional greatness in Henry James' hatred of tyranny; secondly, that there was titanic volume, weight, in the masses he sets in opposition within his work. He uses forces no whit less specifically powerful than the proverbial 'doom of the house' Destiny, *Deus ex machina,* of great traditional art. His art was great art as opposed to over-elaborate or over-refined art by virtue of the major conflicts which he portrays. In his books he showed race against race, immutable; the essential Americanness, or Englishness or Frenchness in *The American,* the difference between one nation and another; not flag-waving and treaties, not the machinery of government, but 'why' there is always misunderstanding, why men of different race are not the same.

We have ceased to believe that we conquer anything by having Alexander the Great make a gigantic 'joy-ride' through India. We know that conquests are made in the laboratory, that Curie with his minute fragments of things seen clearly in test tubes, in curious apparatus, makes conquests. So, too, in these novels, the essential qualities which make up the national qualities, are found and set working, the fundamental oppositions made clear. This is no contemptible labour. No other writer had so assayed three great nations or even thought of attempting it.

Peace comes of communication. No man of our time has so laboured to create means of communication as did the late Henry James. The whole of great art is a struggle for communication. All things that oppose this are evil, whether they be silly scoffing or obstructive tariffs.

And this communication is not a levelling, it is not an elimination of differences. It is a recognition of differences, of the right of differences to exist, of interest in finding things different. Kultur is an abomination; philology is an abomination, all repressive uniforming education is an evil.

From *Literary Essays of Ezra Pound* (Norfolk, Conn.: New Directions, 1954), pp. 295-98.

PERCY LUBBOCK

The Ambassadors

IF IT should still be doubted, however, whether the right use of autobiography is really so limited, it might be a good answer to point to Henry James's Strether, in *The Ambassadors;* Strether may stand as a living demonstration of all that autobiography cannot achieve. He is enough to prove finally how far the intricate performance of thought is beyond the power of a man to record in his own language. Nine-tenths of Strether's thought—nine-tenths, that is to say, of the silvery activity which makes him what he is—would be lost but for the fact that its adventures are caught in time, while they are proceeding, and enacted in the book. Pictured by him, as he might himself look back on them, they would drop to the same plane as the rest of the scene, the picture of the other people in the story; his state of mind would figure in his description on the same terms as the world about him, it would simply be a matter for him to describe like another. In the book as it is, Strether personally has nothing to do with the impression that is made by the mazy career of his imagination, he has no hand in the effect it produces. It speaks for itself, it spreads over the scene and colours the world just as it did for Strether. It is immediately in the foreground, and the "seeing eye" to which it is presented is not his, but the reader's own.

No longer a figure that leans and looks out of a window, scanning a stretch of memory—that is not the image suggested by Henry James's book. It is rather as though the reader himself were at the window, and as though the window opened straight into the depths of Strether's conscious existence. The energy of his perception and discrimination is there seen at work. His mind is the mirror of the scene beyond it, and the other people in the book exist only in relation to him; but his mind, his own thought of them, is there absolutely, its restless evolution is in full sight. I do not say that this is a complete account of the principle on which the book is constructed, for indeed the principle goes further, encompassing points of method to be dealt with later. But for the moment let the book stand as the type of the novel in which a mind is dramatized—reflecting the life to which it is exposed, but itself performing its own peculiar and private life. This last, in the case of Strether, involves a gradual, long-drawn change, from the moment when he takes up the charge of rescuing his young friend from the siren of Paris, to the moment when he finds himself wishing that his young friend would refuse to be rescued. Such is the curve in the unexpected adventure of his imagination. It is given as nobody's view—not his own, as it would be if he told the story himself, and

not the author's, as it would be if Henry James told the story. The author does
not tell the story of Strether's mind; he makes it tell itself, he dramatizes it.

And now for the method by which the picture of a mind is fully dramatized,
the method which is to be seen consistently applied in *The Ambassadors* and
the other later novels of Henry James. How is the author to withdraw, to stand
aside, and to let Strether's thought tell its own story? The thing must be seen
from our own point of view and no other. Author and hero, Thackeray and
Esmond, Meredith and Harry Richmond, have given their various accounts of
emotional and intellectual adventure; but they might do more, they might
bring the facts of the adventure upon the scene and leave them to make their
impression. The story passes in an invisible world, the events take place in the
man's mind; and we might have to conclude that they lie beyond our reach,
and that we cannot attain to them save by the help of the man himself, or of
the author who knows all about him. We might have to make the best of an
account at second hand, and it would not occur to us, I dare say, that anything
more could be forthcoming; we seem to touch the limit of the possibilities of
drama in fiction. But it is not the final limit—there is fiction here to prove
it; and it is this further stroke of the art that I would now examine.

The world of silent thought is thrown open, and instead of telling the reader
what happened there, the novelist uses the look and behaviour of thought as
the vehicle by which the story is rendered. Just as the writer of a play embodies
his subject in visible action and audible speech, so the novelist, dealing with
a situation like Strether's, represents it by means of the movement that flickers
over the surface of his mind. The impulses and reactions of his mood are the
players upon the new scene. In drama of the theatre a character must bear his
part unaided; if he is required to be a desperate man, harbouring thoughts of
crime, he cannot look to the author to appear at the side of the stage and inform
the audience of the fact; he must express it for himself through his words and
deeds, his looks and tones. The playwright so arranges the matter that these
will be enough, the spectator will make the right inference. But suppose that
instead of a man upon the stage, concealing and betraying his thought, we
watch the thought itself, the hidden thing, as it twists to and fro in his
brain—watch it without any other aid to understanding but such as its own
manner of bearing may supply. The novelist, more free than the playwright,
could of course *tell* us, if he chose, what lurks behind this agitated spirit; he
could step forward and explain the restless appearance of the man's thought.
But if he prefers the dramatic way, admittedly the more effective, there is
nothing to prevent him from taking it. The man's thought, in its turn, can
be made to reveal its own inwardness.

Let us see how this plan is pursued in *The Ambassadors*. That book is entirely
concerned with Strether's experience of his peculiar mission to Europe, and
never passes outside the circle of his thought. Strether is despatched, it will
be remembered, by a resolute New England widow, whose son is living lightly
in Paris instead of attending to business at home. To win the hand of the
widow, Strether must succeed in snatching the young man from the siren who
is believed to have beguiled him. The mission is undertaken in all good faith,

Strether descends upon Paris with a mind properly disposed and resolved. He comes as an ambassador representing principle and duty, to treat with the young man, appeal to him convincingly and bear him off. The task before him may be difficult, but his purpose is simple. Strether has reckoned, however, without his imagination; he had scarcely been aware of possessing one before, but everything grows complicated as it is touched and awakened on the new scene. By degrees and degrees he changes his opinion of the life of freedom; it is most unlike his prevision of it, and at last his purpose is actually inverted. He no longer sees a misguided young man to be saved from disaster, he sees an exquisite, bountiful world laid at a young man's feet; and now the only question is whether the young man is capable of meeting and grasping his opportunity. He is incapable, as it turns out; when the story ends he is on the verge of rejecting his freedom and going back to the world of commonplace; Strether's mission has ended successfully. But in Strether's mind the revolution is complete; there is nothing left for him, no reward and no future. The world of commonplace is no longer *his* world, and he is too late to seize the other; he is old, he has missed the opportunity of youth.

This is a story which must obviously be told from Strether's point of view, in the first place. The change in his purpose is due to a change in his vision, and the long slow process could not be followed unless his vision were shared by the reader. Strether's predicament, that is to say, could not be placed upon the stage; his outward behaviour, his conduct, his talk, do not express a tithe of it. Only the brain behind his eyes can be aware of the colour of his experience, as it passes through its innumerable gradations; and all understanding of his case depends upon seeing these. The way of the author, therefore, who takes this subject in hand, is clear enough at the outset. It is a purely pictorial subject, covering Strether's field of vision and bounded by its limits; it consists entirely of an impression received by a certain man. There can accordingly be no thought of rendering him as a figure seen from without; nothing that any one else could discern, looking at him and listening to his conversation, would give the full sense of the eventful life he is leading within. The dramatic method, as we ordinarily understand it, is ruled out at once. Neither as an action set before the reader without interpretation from within, nor yet as an action pictured for the reader by some other onlooker in the book, can this story possibly be told.

Strether's real situation, in fact, is not his open and visible situation, between the lady in New England and the young man in Paris; his grand adventure is not expressed in its incidents. These, as they are devised by the author, are secondary, they are the extension of the moral event that takes place in the breast of the ambassador, his change of mind. That is the very middle of the subject; it is a matter that lies solely between Strether himself and his vision of the free world. It is a delightful effect of irony, indeed, that he should have accomplished his errand after all, in spite of himself; but the point of the book is not there, the ironic climax only serves to bring out the point more sharply. The reversal of his own idea is underlined and enhanced by the reversal of the young man's idea in the opposite sense; but essentially the subject of the book would be unchanged if the story ended differently, if the young man held to his freedom and refused to go home. Strether would still have passed through the same cycle of unexpected experience; his errand might have failed, but still it would not have been any the more impossible for him to claim his reward, for his part, than it is impossible as things are, with the quest achieved and the young man ready to hasten back to duty of his own accord. And so the subject can only be reached through Strether's consciousness, it is plain; that way alone will command the impression that the scene makes on him. Nothing in the scene has any importance, any value in itself; what Strether sees in it—that is the whole of its meaning.

But though in *The Ambassadors* the point of view is primarily Strether's, and though it *appears* to be his throughout the book, there is in fact an insidious shifting of it, so artfully contrived that the reader may arrive at the end without suspecting the trick. The reader, all unawares, is placed in a better position for an understanding of Strether's history, better than the position of Strether himself. Using his eyes, we see what *he* sees, we are possessed of the material on which his patient thought sets to work; and that is so far well enough, and plainly necessary. All the other people in the book face towards him, and it is that aspect of them, and that only, which is shown to the reader; still more important, the beautiful picture of Paris and spring-time, the stir and shimmer of life in the Rue de Rivoli and the gardens of the Tuileries, is Strether's picture, *his* vision, rendered as the time and the place strike upon his senses. All this on which his thought ruminates, the stuff that occupies it, is represented from his point of view. To see it, even for a moment, from some different angle if, for example, the author interposed with a vision of his own would patently disturb the right impression. The author does no such thing, it need hardly be said.

When it comes to Strether's treatment of this material, however, when it is time to learn what he makes of it, turning his experience over and over in his mind, then his own point of view no longer serves. How is anybody, even Strether, to *see* the working of his own mind? A mere account of its working, after the fact, has already been barred; we have found that this of necessity is lacking in force, it is statement where we look for demonstration. And so we must see for ourselves, the author must so arrange matters that Strether's thought will all be made intelligible by a direct view of its surface. The immediate flaw or ripple of the moment, and the next and the next, will then take up the tale, like the speakers in a dialogue which gradually unfolds the subject of the play. Below the surface, behind the outer aspect of his mind, we do not penetrate; this is drama, and in drama the spectator must judge by appearances. When Strether's mind is dramatized, nothing is shown but the passing images that anybody might detect, looking down upon a mind grown visible. There is no drawing upon extraneous sources of information; Henry James knows all there is to know of Strether, but he most carefully refrains from using his knowledge. He wishes us to accept nothing from him, on authority—only to watch and learn.

For suppose him to begin sharing the knowledge that he alone possesses, as the author and inventor of Strether; suppose that instead of representing only the momentary appearance of Strether's thought he begins to expound its substance: he must at once give us the whole of it, must let us into every secret without delay, or his exposition is plainly misleading. It is assumed that he tells all, if he once begins. And so, too, if the book were cast autobiographically and Strether spoke in person; he could not hold back, he could not heighten the story of his thought with that touch of suspense, waiting to be resolved, which stamps the impression so firmly into the memory of the onlooker. In a tale of murder and mystery there is one man who cannot possibly be the narrator, and that is the murderer himself; for if he admits us into his mind at all he must do so without reserve, thereby betraying the secret that we ought to be guessing at for ourselves. But by this method of *The Ambassadors* the mind of which the reader is made free, Strether's mind, is not given away; there is no need for it to yield up all its secrets at once. The story in it is played out by due degrees, and there may be just as much deliberation, refrainment, suspension, as in a story told scenically upon the stage. All the effect of true drama is thus at the disposal of the author, even when he seems to be describing and picturing the consciousness of one of his characters. He arrives at the point where apparently nothing but a summary and a report should be possible, and even there he is precluded from none of the privileges of a dramatist.

It is necessary to show that in his attitude towards his European errand Strether is slowly turning upon himself and looking in another direction. To announce the fact, with a tabulation of his reasons, would be the historic, retrospective, undramatic way of dealing with the matter. To bring his mind into view at the different moments, one after another, when it is brushed by new experience—to make a little scene of it, without breaking into hidden depths where the change of purpose is proceeding—to multiply these glimpses until the silent change is apparent, though no word has actually been said of it: this is Henry James's way, and though the *method* could scarcely be more devious and roundabout, always refusing the short cut, yet by these very qualities and precautions it finally produces the most direct impression, for the reader has *seen*. That is why the method is adopted. The author has so fashioned his book that his own part in the narration is now unobtrusive to the last degree; he, the author, could not imaginably figure there more discreetly. His part in the effect is no more than that of the playwright, who vanishes and leaves his people to act the story; only instead of men and women talking together, in Strether's case there are innumerable images of thought crowding across the stage, expressing the story in their behaviour.

But there is more in the book, as I suggested just now, than Strether's vision and the play of his mind. In the *scenic* episodes, the colloquies that Strether holds, for example, with his sympathetic friend Maria Gostrey, another turn appears in the author's procedure. Throughout these clear-cut dialogues Strether's point of view still reigns; the only eyes in the matter are still his, there is no sight of the man himself as his companion sees him. Miss Gostrey is clearly visible, and Madame de Vionnet and little Bilham, or whoever it may be; the face of Strether himself is never turned to the reader. On the evening of the first encounter between the elderly ambassador and the young man, they sat together in a cafe of the boulevards and walked away at midnight through quiet streets; and all through their interview the fact of the young man's appearance is strongly dominant, for it is this that first reveals to Strether how the young man has been transformed by his commerce with the free world; and so his figure is sharply before the reader as they talk. How Strether seemed to Chad—this, too, is represented, but only by implication, through Chad's speech and manner. It is essential, of course, that it should be so, the one-sided vision is strictly enjoined by the method of the whole book. But though the seeing eye is still with Strether, there is a noticeable change in the author's way with him.

In these scenic dialogues, on the whole, we seem to have edged away from Strether's consciousness. He sees, and we with him; but when he *talks* it is almost as though we were outside him and away from him altogether. Not always, indeed; for in many of the scenes he is busily brooding and thinking throughout, and we share his mind while he joins in the talk. But still, on the whole, the author is inclined to leave Strether alone when the scene is set. He talks the matter out with Maria, he sits and talks with Madame de Vionnet, he strolls along the boulevards with Chad, he lounges on a chair in the Champs Elysées with some one else—we know the kind of scene that is set for Strether, know how very few accessories he requires, and know that the scene marks a certain definite climax, wherever it occurs, for all its everyday look. The occasion is important, there is no doubt about that; its importance is in the air. And Strether takes his part in it as though he had almost become what he cannot be, an objective figure for the reader. Evidently he cannot be that, since the centre of vision is still within him; but by an easy sleight of hand the author gives him almost the value of an independent person, a man to whose words we may listen expectantly, a man whose mind is screened from us. Again and again the stroke is accomplished, and indeed there is nothing mysterious about it. Simply it consists in treating the scene as dramatically as possible—keeping it framed in Strether's vision, certainly, but keeping his consciousness out of sight, his thought unexplored. He talks to Maria; and to us, to the reader, his voice seems as much as hers to belong to somebody whom we are *watching*—which is impossible, because our point of view is his.

A small matter, perhaps, but it is interesting as a sign, still another, of the perpetual tendency of the novel to capture the advantages which it appears to forego. *The Ambassadors* is without doubt a book that deals with an entirely nondramatic subject; it is the picture of an *état d'âme*. But just as the chapters that are concerned with Strether's soul are in the key of drama, after the fashion I have described, so too the episode, the occasion, the scene that crowns the impression, is always more dramatic in its method than it apparently has the means to be. Here, for instance, is the central scene of the whole story, the scene in the old Parisian garden, where Strether, finally filled to the brim with the sensation of all the life for which his own opportunity has passed, overflows with his passionate exhortation to little Bilham warning him, adjuring him not to make *his* mistake, not to let life slide away ungrasped. It is the hour in which

Strether touches his crisis, and the first necessity of the chapter is to show the sudden lift and heave of his mood within; the voices and admonitions of the hour, that is to say, must be heard and felt as he hears and feels them himself. The scene, then, will be given as Strether's impression, clearly, and so it is; the old garden and the evening light and the shifting company of people appear as their reflection in his thought. But the scene is *also* a piece of drama, it strikes out of the book with the strong relief of dramatic action; which is evidently an advantage gained, seeing the importance of the hour in the story, but which is an advantage that it could not enjoy, one might have said.

The quality of the scene becomes clear if we imagine the story to be told by Strether himself, narrating in the first person. Of the damage that this would entail for the picture of his brooding mind I have spoken already; but suppose the book to have taken the form of autobiography, and suppose that Strether has brought the story up to this point, where he sits beside little Bilham in Gloriani's garden. He describes the deep and agitating effect of the scene upon him, calling to him of the world he has missed; he tells what he thought and felt; and then, he says, I broke out with the following tirade to little Bilham and we have the energetic outburst which Henry James has put into his mouth. But is it not clear how the incident would be weakened, so rendered? That speech, word for word as we have it, would lose its unexpected and dramatic quality, because Strether, arriving at it by narration, could not suddenly spring away from himself and give the impression of the worn, intelligent, clear-sighted man sitting there in the evening sun, strangely moved to unwonted eloquence. His narration must have discounted the effect of his outburst, leading us up to the very edge of it, describing how it arose, explaining where it came from. He would be *subjective,* and committed to remain so all the time.

Henry James, by his method, can secure this effect of drama, even though his Strether is apparently in the position of a narrator throughout. Strether's are the eyes, I said, and they are more so than ever during this hour in the garden; he is the sentient creature in the scene. But the author, who all through the story has been treating Strether's consciousness as a play, as an action proceeding, can at any moment use his talk almost as though the source from which it springs were unknown to us from within. I remember that he himself, in his critical preface to the book, calls attention to the way in which a conversation between Strether and Maria Gostrey, near the beginning, puts the reader in possession of all the past facts of the situation which it is necessary for him to know; a *scene* thus takes the place of that "harking back to make up," as he calls it, which is apt to appear as a lump of narrative shortly after the opening of a story. If Strether were really the narrator, whether in the first person or the third, he could not use his own talk in this manner; he would have to tell us himself about his past. But he has never *told* us his thought, we have looked at it and drawn our inferences; and so there is still some air of dramatic detachment about him, and his talk may seem on occasion to be that of a man whom we know from outside. The advantage is peculiarly felt on that crucial occasion at Gloriani's, where Strether's sudden flare of vehemence, so natural and yet so unlike him, breaks out with force unimpaired. It strikes freshly on the ear, the speech of a man whose inmost perturbations we have indeed inferred from many glimpses of his mind, but still without ever learning the full tale of them from himself.

The Ambassadors, then, is a story which is seen from one man's point of view, and yet a story in which that point of view is itself a matter for the reader to confront and to watch constructively. Everything in the novel is now dramatically rendered, whether it is a page of dialogue or a page of description, because even in the page of description nobody is addressing us, nobody is reporting his impression to the reader. The impression is enacting itself in the endless series of images that play over the outspread expanse of the man's mind and memory. When the story passes from these to the scenes of dialogue from the silent drama of Strether's meditation to the spoken drama of the men and women there is thus no break in the method. The same law rules everywhere that Strether's changing sense of his situation shall appeal directly to the onlooker, and not by way of any summarizing picture-maker. And yet *as a whole* the book is all pictorial, an indirect impression received through Strether's intervening consciousness, beyond which the story never strays. I conclude that on this paradox the art of dramatizing the picture of somebody's experience— the art I have been considering in these last chapters—touches its limit. There is indeed no further for it to go.

From *The Craft of Fiction* (London: Jonathan Cape, 1921), pp. 145-47, 156-71.

VAN WYCK BROOKS

From *The Pilgrimage of Henry James*

A HISTORIAN of manners, a critic of manners, a mind at home with itself, alert, witty, instructed, in its own familiar domain. Yes, and in the foreground of life, the ground of the typical, the general. Turgenev said of Flaubert's Monsieur Homais that the great strength of such a portrait consisted in its being at once an individual, of the most concrete sort, and a type. James creates these types again and again: they are not universal but they are national—there are scarcely half a dozen figures in American fiction to be placed beside them. Christopher Newman remains for all time the wistful American business man who spends his life hankering after the fine things he has missed. Daisy Miller's character, predicament, life, and death are the story of a whole phase of the social history of America. Dr. Sloper, that perfect embodiment of the respectability of old New York; Miss Birdseye, the symbol of the aftermath of the heroic age of New England; Mrs. Burrage, the eternal New York hostess; Gilbert Osmond, the Italianate American—these are all veritable creations: indeed one has only to recall Winterbourne, in *Daisy Miller,* the American who has lived abroad so long that he has ceased to understand the behavior of his fellow country-woman, to perceive with what an unfailing resourcefulness James infuses into the least of his characters the element of the typical. It goes without saying that all this, together with the tenderness and the benevolent humor that bathe the primitive Jamesian scene, indicates the sort of understanding that is born only of race. These novels are the work of a man who was so sure of his world that he could play with it as all the great novelists have played with their worlds. The significant theme came to him with a natural inevitability, for he shared some of the deepest and most characteristic desires of his compatriots. And this relation, as long as he maintained it, endowed him with the notes of the great tellers of tales, the note of the satirist, the note of the idyllist, the note of the tragedian. . . .

He had emerged as an impassioned geometer—or, shall we say, some vast arachnid of art, pouncing upon the tiny air-blown particle and wrapping it round and round. And now a new prodigy had appeared, a style, the style that was the man Henry James had become. He had eschewed the thin, the sharp, the meagre; he had desired the rich, the round, the resonant, and all these things had been added unto him; everything that he had thought and felt and tasted and touched, the fabrics upon which his eyes had feasted, the colors that he had loved, the soft sounds, the delicate scents, had left their stamp upon the house of his spirit. The house?—he had "thrown out extensions and protrusions, indulging even, all recklessly, in gables and pinnacles and battle-ments, things that had transformed the unpretending place into a veritable palace, an extravagant, bristling, flag-flying structure that had quite as much to do with the air 'as with the earth." His sense, like Adam Verver's, had been kept sharp, year after year, by the collation of types and signs, the comparison of fine object with fine object, of one degree of finish, of one form of the exquisite with another; and type and object and form had moulded his style. Metaphors bloomed there like tropical air-plants, throwing out branches and flowers; and every sound was muted and every motion vague.

For other things had passed into this style—the evasiveness, the hesitancy, the scrupulosity of an habitually embarrassed man. The caution, the ceremoni-ousness, the baffled curiosity, the nervousness and constant self-communion, the fear of committing himself—these traits of the self-conscious guest in the house where he had never been at home had fashioned with time the texture of his personality. They had infected the creatures of his fancy, they had fixed the character of his imaginative world; and behind his novels, those formidable projections of a geometrical intellect, were to be discerned now the confused reveries of an invalid child. For in his prolonged association with people who had merely glimmered for him, in the constant abrogation of his moral judg-ment, in these years of an enchanted exile in a museum-world—for what else had England ever been for him?—Henry James had reverted to a kind of childhood. Plots thronged through his mind, dim figures which, like his own Chad and Strether, "passed each other, in their deep immersion, with the round, impersonal eye of silent fish"; and with these figures, as with pawns or paper soldiers, he devised his labyrinthine games. What interested him was not the figures but their relations, the relations which alone make pawns significant.

From *The Pilgrimage of Henry James* (London: Jonathan Cape, 1928), pp. 102-103, 130-32.

EDITH WHARTON

The Artist

IT IS particularly regrettable in the case of Henry James that no one among his intimates had a recording mind, or rather that those who had did not apply it to noting down his conversation, for I have never known a case in which an author's talk and his books so enlarged and supplemented each other. Talent is often like an ornamental excrescence; but the quality loosely called genius usually irradiates the whole character. "If he but so much as cut his nails," was Goethe's homely phrase of Schiller, "one saw at once that he was a greater man than any of them." This irradiation, so abundantly basked in by the friends of Henry James, was hidden from those who knew him slightly by a peculiarity due to merely physical causes. His slow way of speech, sometimes mistaken for affectation—or, more quaintly, for an artless form of Anglomania!—was really the partial victory over a stammer which in his boyhood had been thought incurable. The elaborate politeness and the involved phraseology that made off-hand intercourse with him so difficult to casual acquaintances probably sprang from the same defect. To have too much time in which to weigh each word before uttering it could not but lead, in the case of the alertest and most sensitive of minds, to self-consciousness and self-criticism; and this fact explains the hesitating manner that often passed for a mannerism. Once, in New York, when I had arranged a meeting between him and the great Mr. Dooley, whose comments on the world's ways he greatly enjoyed, I perceived, as I watched them after dinner, that Peter Dunne was floundering helplessly in the heavy seas of James's parentheses; and the next time we met, after speaking of his delight in having at last seen James, he added mournfully: "What a pity it takes him so long to say anything! Everything he said was so splendid but I felt like telling him all the time: 'Just 'pit it right up into Popper's hand'."

To James's intimates, however, these elaborate hesitancies, far from being an obstacle, were like a cobweb bridge flung from his mind to theirs, an invisible passage over which one knew that silver-footed ironies, veiled jokes, tiptoe malices, were stealing to explode a huge laugh at one's feet. This moment of suspense, in which there was time to watch the forces of malice and merriment assembling over the mobile landscape of his face, was perhaps the rarest of all in the unique experience of a talk with Henry James.

His letters, delightful as they are, give but hints and fragments of his talk; the talk that, to his closest friends, when his health and the surrounding conditions were favourable, poured out in a series of images so vivid and appreciations so penetrating, the whole so sunned over by irony, sympathy and wide-flashing fun, that those who heard him at his best will probably agree in saying of him what he once said to me of M. Paul Bourget: "He was the first, easily, of all the talkers I ever encountered." . . .

I one day said to him: "What was your idea in suspending the four principal characters in 'The Golden Bowl' in the void? What sort of life did they lead when they were not watching each other, and fencing with each other? Why have you stripped them of all the *human fringes* we necessarily trail after us through life?"

He looked at me in surprise, and I saw at once that the surprise was painful, and wished I had not spoken. I had assumed that his system was a deliberate one, carefully thought out, and had been genuinely anxious to hear his reasons. But after a pause of reflection he answered in a disturbed voice: "My dear I didn't know I had!" and I saw that my question, instead of starting one of our absorbing literary discussions, had only turned his startled attention on a peculiarity of which he had been completely unconscious.

This sensitiveness to criticism or comment of any sort had nothing to do with vanity; it was caused by the great artist's deep consciousness of his powers, combined with a bitter, a life-long disappointment at his lack of popular recognition. I am not sure that Henry James had not secretly dreamed of being a "best seller" in the days when that odd form of literary fame was at its height; at any rate he certainly suffered all his life and more and more as time went on from the lack of recognition among the very readers who had most warmly welcomed his early novels. He could not understand why the success achieved by "Daisy Miller" and "The Portrait of a Lady" should be denied to the great novels of his maturity: and the sense of protracted failure made him miserably alive to the least hint of criticism, even from those who most completely understood, and sympathized with, his later experiments in technique and style.

From *A Backward Glance* (New York: Appleton-Century, 1934), pp. 177-79, 191-92.

YVOR WINTERS

Henry James' Moral Sense

THE MOTIVATING ideas of most of the novels of Henry James might be summarized very briefly, and perhaps a trifle crudely, as follows: that there is a moral sense, a sense of decency, inherent in human character at its best; that this sense of decency, being only a sense, exists precariously, and may become confused and even hysterical in a crisis; that it may be enriched and cultivated through association with certain environments; that such association may, also, be carried so far as to extinguish the moral sense. This last relationship, that of the moral sense to an environment which may up to a certain point enrich it and beyond that point dissolve it, resembles the ordinary relationship of intellect to experience, of character to sensibility.

If we carry these generalizations a little farther into the specific terms of his novels, we find, however: that the moral sense as James conceives it is essentially American or at least appears to James most clearly in American character; that it can be cultivated by association with European civilization and manners; that it may be weakened or in some other manner betrayed by an excess of such association.

Superficially this description seems to omit the novels of the brief middle period, in which most of the characters were British and in which none were American; but actually these novels are in nearly every case constructed in much the same terms, for the "American" characteristics are given to certain personages, and the "European" to certain others. This formula will be somewhat qualified as we proceed, but I believe that it is essentially sound.

Now this particular kind of moral sense may have existed in Europe as well as in America, but so far as James was concerned, it was essentially an American phenomenon: in the first place, I believe that I shall be able to show how a degree of intensity of this moral sense was an actual and historical development in the American context; in the second place, we have in James the ultimate and rarefied development of the spiritual antagonism which had existed for centuries between the rising provincial civilization and the richer civilization from which it had broken away, an antagonism in which the provincial civilization met the obviously superior cultivation of the parent with a more or less typically provincial assertion of moral superiority. The same theme obsesses Fenimore Cooper for a large portion of his career, though conceived in terms less subtle; it is the same antagonism which, from pre-Revolutionary days to the present, has resulted in the attempt, unhealthy in its self-consciousness and in its neurotic intensity, to create a literature which shall be utterly independent of that of England; it is the same antagonism which has led many of the compatriots of Henry James to disown him as a foreigner because of his long residence abroad, and which led his western contemporaries of the intellectual stamp of Clemens to despise James in turn for his cultivation and artistry. There is further evidence that James conceived this moral sense to be essentially American, moreover, in the fact that the moral phenomenon and its attendant dramatic formula alike were first defined in the early American period of his art, and that they were most fully and richly developed in his last great masterpieces, *The Ambassadors, The Wings of the Dove,* and *The Golden Bowl.*

The origin of this moral sense may be given briefly and with fair certainty, though James himself nowhere defines it: it was the product of generations of discipline in the ethical systems of the Roman Catholic and Anglo-Catholic Churches, a product which subsisted as a traditional way of feeling and of acting after the ideas which had formed it, and which, especially in Europe and before the settlement of America, had long supported it, had ceased to be understood, or, as ideas, valued. The Anglo-Catholic Church in New York and farther south, even before the Revolutionary War, tended to rely upon society for its support, rather than to support society; it was the external sign of the respectability of a class, and was scarcely an evangelizing or an invigorating force. . . .

The foregoing pages might lead the careless reader to assume that my opinion of James is low; the fact of the matter is, that if I were permitted a definition of the novel which should exclude among other works *Moby Dick, Mardi, The Encantadas,* and the autobiographical works of Melville—and such a definition would be neither difficult nor illegitimate—I should be inclined to consider James as the greatest novelist in English, as he is certainly one of the five or six greatest writers of any variety to be produced in North America, though the estimate would proceed from a view of the history and form of the novel that would in all likelihood be pleasing to few devotees of that art.

The fact of the matter is, that in reading most of the English and American novelists preceding James who are commonly conceded to be great, our estimate of the writers' genius is formed very largely on the quality of the incidentals of the works under consideration, and not on the quality of what in a drama or an epic would be the essentials. Jane Austen, who is inescapably one of the best, hangs her remarkably brilliant comment and characterization on frames of action so conventional as to be all but trivial; the same is true of Trollope; it is more obviously true of Scott. It is less true of such a writer as Dickens, but a plot by Dickens, and usually half of the attendant characters, will ordinarily be so corrupted by insufferable sentimentalism, that one turns hither and yonder infallibly to reap what profit one may from the details. The plotting of Meredith and of George Eliot is far more serious, but both writers fall very much below James in characterization and in the quality of their prose. The prose of James is sometimes obscure, and as a result of the obscurity it may sometimes be found diffuse, but it is always sensitive and honest; the prose of George Eliot is laborious, and the prose of Meredith is worse—it is laboriously clever.

If we come to James as we come to Dickens or to Trollope, with the initial assumption that the plot can be taken or left according to the mood of the reader, the wealth of incidental felicities which we are likely to find will scarcely be equalled by any other novelist in English. Many writers have commented upon the unforgettable vividness of James's characterization; I personally have a far sharper recollection of the characteristics and attitudes, even of the external appearance, of many characters from James, and I have such a recollection of more characters, than I have from all the rest of English fiction, and certainly far more than I have from my own life. . . .

Further, the margin of imperfection in many of the works is not of the utmost seriousness aesthetically. Many of the minor works—*The Europeans* is nearly the best example—are perfect within their limits; the margin of difficulty in such major efforts as *The Portrait of a Lady* and *The Ambassadors* is not great in proportion to the wealth offered us; *The Wings of the Dove* and *The Golden Bowl,* though both books display undue clairvoyance on the part of certain characters, are both in their central plotting, it seems to me, perfectly sound.

Finally, his very virtues, in the semi-successful works, and in the successful as well, are closely related to his defects. His defects arise from the effort on the part of the novelist and of his characters to understand ethical problems in a pure state, and to understand them absolutely, to examine the marginal, the semi-obscure, the fine and definitive boundary of experience; the purely moral—that is, the moral divorced from all problems of manners and of compulsion, as it appears in the case of Fleda Vetch—can probably be defined but very rarely, and more or less as the result of good fortune in regard to the given facts of the situation, with the precision which James appears to seek, so that the effort in all save a few occasional and perfect situations must necessarily lead to more or less supersubtlety, and if the supersubtlety is pushed far enough, as it sometimes is, to an obscurantism amounting in effect to hallucination. On the other hand, the effort unquestionably results in a degree of very genuine subtlety, not only of central moral perception, but of incidental perception of character, that no other novelist has equalled. An additional reason for the memorableness of the Jamesian characters is the seriousness with which they take themselves and each other: we feel that we are somehow on essential ground with them, even if the essentiality of the ground results in its shifting like quicksand; we may disapprove of Fleda Vetch as a person for her errors and as a creation for the errors of James; but the integrity with which the errors are made, their fidelity to the historical context of which they are an essential part, and in spite of the fact that a great artist properly considered ought to have a better understanding than James displayed of the defects and dangers of his own historical context, this integrity and this fidelity in themselves are unforgettable; we do not have great tragedy, but we at least share a real experience, and the reality is of a quality that we shall find but rarely if at all in other novelists. And finally, we have only the loosest conception of the successful works and elements of James, if we do not fully understand his kind and degree of failure, for the failure represents the particular problem with which he was struggling to deal—one could almost regard it as his subject-matter.

From *Maule's Curse* (Norfolk, Conn.: New Directions, 1938), pp. 169-71, 208-11.

F. O. MATTHIESSEN

The Golden Bowl

SOME OF the consequences of the industrial revolution are oddly refracted in *The Golden Bowl*. The Ververs' wealth is of the new kind. To be sure, the product of Woollett, which Strether fastidiously refused to specify for Maria, was turned out by a New England factory that was on its way to establishing a monopoly. But the Newsomes' family fortune was only a background for James' main theme. And when money became the great tempter for Kate Croy, the source of Milly's fabulous inheritance was left entirely shrouded. Adam Verver's fortune, on the other hand, has been made entirely by himself in the post Civil War west. His again unspecified financial dealings have been as rapid as they have been vast, since he is only forty-seven, with retirement several years behind him. But he has brought his acquisitive sense into his leisure. Like so many other robber barons, he has set his heart on becoming a great collector, and gold and jewel images color, in consequence, every relationship in the novel.

Since James, not Balzac or Dreiser, is the author, most of these images have aesthetic rather than commercial connotations. They constitute the high-water mark of James' virtuosity. In the opening chapter, which presents Prince Amerigo on the eve of his marriage to Maggie Verver, the young Italian thinks of the golden bath in which he is about to be immersed as having far greater dimensions than any that had ever been supplied by the imperial loot of his remote ancestors. In Mr. Verver's view, the Prince himself is a collector's item, a costly specimen of the *cinquecento*. The book shines throughout with innumerable other such images. In two of James' most breath-takingly elaborate efforts the Prince is at one time a Palladian church, at another a dazzling pagoda. Maggie Verver becomes, to her father's eye, a lovely sculptured figure, though he is a bit vague as to whether she is a nymph or a nun. To a much greater extent than even James had previously sought for, entire scenes are centered around pictures and *objets d'art*. The culmination of this tendency is the treatment of the golden bowl.

The method of introducing and developing this symbol is the same as for the wings of the dove, though both extended and intensified. The scene in which the Prince and Charlotte Stant discover the bowl in an antique shop, while supposedly looking for a wedding present for Maggie, makes the ending of the first book. The two long chapters which lead up to and away from Mrs. Assingham's dashing the bowl to the floor form not only the climax to the fourth book, but also the most dramatic moment in the novel. It may be observed, parenthetically, that the division into books is less important here than in either *The Ambassadors* or *The Wings of the Dove*. That is not to say that James was less concerned with composition, since, as though challenged by all the works of art that he had conjured up, he bent every effort to making his structure architectural in its rigorous symmetry. The first half centers around the Prince, the second half around the Princess. The division of each half into three books marks, in the first instance, necessary lapses of time. Between the first and second books a sufficient interval must have passed since the Prince's marriage to Maggie to make her feel that her father is too much alone and that he ought to marry again. Between the second and third books Mr. Verver's marriage with Charlotte has taken place, and Maggie has finally begun to awaken to the situation between Charlotte and the Prince. At this point the whole *donnée* is before us, as it was not in the slowly evolving two previous novels. Everything is now concentrated upon Maggie's effort to win back her husband. The pace is much swifter. There are no further lapses of time. The fourth book, which occupies over half of the second volume, takes us to the moment when Maggie confronts the Prince with her knowledge. By the end of the fifth book she has triumphed over Charlotte, and the sixth book is needed only for a brief conclusion, to dispatch Mr. Verver and Charlotte back to America.

James uses the bowl as a means of bringing to a focal point the varying and diverging complexities in such human relations. He gives no indication whether he was thinking of Blake's cryptic verses:

> Can wisdom be kept in a silver rod,
> Or love in a golden bowl?

But that latter question is insistent throughout. When the antique dealer shows the bowl to Charlotte, her first comment is: 'It may be cheap for what it is, but it will be dear, I'm afraid, for me.' We think at once of what has been too dear for her, of the fact that, despite her love for the Prince, their marriage had been out of the question because of their lack of means. The Prince is thus the golden bowl, the 'pure and perfect crystal' which Mr. Verver has been happy to pay a big price for. But the bowl itself is quickly seen to have a flaw, and so it becomes a symbol rather for the relationship between the Prince and Charlotte—significantly he detects at once the crack beneath the gilt surface, whereas she is blind to it. Such a gift will never do for Maggie, and so they drop their pursuit, each with a refusal also to accept from the other any memento of their now dead past. They are acting here in good faith, and when he tells her that she too must marry, she answers, in the concluding lines of the first book: 'Well, I would marry, I think, to have something from you in all freedom.'

By the time of the reintroduction of the theme of the bowl, these words have taken on irony. Charlotte is married to Mr. Verver, and the old absorbing intimacy of father and daughter has thrown the other two continually by themselves. The day in the country when they finally take full advantage of their freedom is figured by the Prince as 'a great gold cup that we must somehow drain together.' A similar sounding of the theme is made by Maggie when, waking to the loss of her husband, she speaks of 'the full cup' of her need of him. But the most brilliant demonstration in all James' work of what he could do with a symbol is in those two climactic scenes, between Maggie and Fanny Assingham, and then between Maggie and the Prince. Maggie herself has now stumbled upon the bowl while looking for a remembrance for her father's birthday; and from certain details that the dealer unwittingly let fall, she has pieced together the earlier scene in his shop, and has seen the bowl as the sign of her husband's intimacy with Charlotte. She has placed it in the center of her mantel to confront him as soon as he comes in, but now that she feels her whole future to be weighted by the bowl, she has a foreboding that perhaps the Prince may never again enter her room. Mrs. Assingham, who has known about the others' relation, but has been determined to keep it from Maggie, tells her that her whole idea 'has a crack,' just as the bowl has. Insisting that nothing stands between Maggie and the Prince, she dramatically smashes the bowl on the polished floor. How thoroughly James' imagination was imbued with the devices of the fairy story is attested by the fact that the Prince instantly appears, just as though he was a genie released by the breaking of an evil spell. Though that comparison is not made, such is the effect.

As Maggie gathers up the three pieces into which the bowl has split, the two halves of the cup itself and 'the solid detached foot,' the urgent question for her is what can be salvaged from the triangle in which she is involved. The bowl is now the token of her knowledge, of the fact that she hasn't been such an innocent fool as the Prince may have supposed. As she confronts him with this, the dawning possibility of his new need of her seems to flicker over the fragments. The dramatic 'thickness' of such scenes can obviously not be paraphrased, since their excitement depends on the ranging play of association that is in the air at every moment. The Prince and Maggie are talking about the actual bowl, but other meanings are more shiftingly alive:

"And what, pray, *was* the price?"

She paused again a little. "It was high certainly for those fragments. I think I feel as I look at them there rather ashamed to say."

The Prince then again looked at them; he might have been growing used to the sight. "But shall you at least get your money back?"

That remains the crucial question for the rest of the novel, whether the Ververs have paid too much for their Prince. As Maggie says to Mrs. Assingham, she wants 'the golden bowl as it *was* to have been . . . The bowl with all our happiness in it. The bowl without the crack.' By the end that is what she has gained. In the closing scene James again finds his own kind of use for a work of art. Maggie and her father are commenting on the fineness of 'the early Florentine sacred subject' that he had given her on her marriage; but as they look at the picture, they are really exchanging views on the resolution of the situation. When Mr. Verver says, '*Le compte y est.* You've got some good things,' the Prince falls under his glance as the best attestation 'of a rare power of purchase.' And when Maggie and her husband are left alone at last, the mingled images of beauty and wealth are still sustained. She reflects that here is 'the golden fruit that had shone from afar.' But the gold is more substantial than that. She knows now that she is going 'to be paid in full.' As the Prince turns to her for their final embrace, he 'might have been holding out the money bag for her to come and take it.'

The expertness with which James has brought out so many connotations latent in the bowl has kept that symbol from ever becoming frozen or schematized. He has thus unquestionably succeeded in making an *objet d'art* the cohesive center of his own intricate creation. But other questions are raised by those curiously mixed final images. When there is so much gold that it pervades even the vocabulary of love, is that a sign of life or of death? What sort of world is being portrayed, and how are we to judge it?

In the view of Colonel Assingham, the most detached observer here, life is largely 'a matter of pecuniary arrangement,' and Maggie Verver is 'more than anything else the young woman who has a million a year.' But the American world into which he is launched is far less simple for the Prince. He figures it, through his early memory of Poe's *Narrative of A. Gordon Pym,* as 'a dazzling curtain of light, concealing as darkness conceals, yet of the colour of milk or of snow.' He has been used to curtains of black and doesn't know what to expect in Maggie's realm of moral innocence, where the very existence of evil seems to be lost in the shrouding 'white mist.' That Americans are 'incredibly romantic,' he avows to her at the start. 'Of course we are,' she answers. 'That's just what makes everything so nice for us.'

James has clearly bent his attention to showing how nice that can be. He has continued down the vistas that opened for him in *The Wings of the Dove.* The Ververs are far richer even than Milly Theale; and if she was a pretended princess, Maggie Verver's marriage has made her an actual one. More than that, her father is virtually a king: he is likened to Alexander 'furnished with the spoils of Darius.' The character most comparable to Adam Verver in James' earlier work is Christopher Newman, in *The American,* and that comparison is instructive for James' development. The first names of both men call attention to the quality that James was most concerned to endow them with: both are discoverers of new worlds, just as, in turn, Prince Amerigo's name symbolizes how he must be a re-discoverer of America, or of what may prove even harder, of Americans. What Newman and Mr. Verver also have in common is their newness: it would hardly seem accidental that both syllables of the latter's surname suggest spring. Both too have had their moments of vision in which the mere amassing of money came to seem futile. An amusing corroboration of the exorbitant demands raised by James' later imagination is that the financial deal which brought home that truth to Newman was originally for sixty thousand dollars, but was changed in the revision to half a million. But whereas Newman came to Europe with a quiet eagerness for wider experience, Mr. Verver brought along his far vaster fortune and a scheme. His 'business of the future' was 'to rifle the Golden Isles.' He might, like James himself, have been a friend of Mrs. Jack Gardner's, so typical was his desire of our era of 'the pillage of the past,' as Lewis Mumford has called it. Mr. Verver's vision, his 'peak in Darien,' as James calls it, has stretched out before him the gleaming possibility of giving to his home town, American City, situated somewhat dimly beyond the Mississippi, a whole museum complete with contents. He has reached even as far as Henry Ford was going to: he would like even to transport 'the little old church' from his English estate 'for its simple sweetness.' Never, indeed, have the claims of the collector been pitched higher: he conceives his dedicated role 'as equal somehow' to that of 'the great seers, the invokers and encouragers of beauty—and he didn't after all perhaps dangle so far below the great producers and creators.'

The odd thing is that James seems to take Mr. Verver at his own estimate. Furthermore, though he posits for him an 'acquisitive power' that amounted to 'a special genius,' James deliberately invests him also with a paradisal innocence. He is simplicity incarnate. In contrast with the flamboyant architectural images for the Prince, his face suggests 'a small decent room, clean-swept.' Seated at the head of his table, he is 'like a little boy shyly entertaining in virtue of some imposed rank . . . quite as an infant king is the representative of a dynasty.' He seems at times even more youthful than the Principino, his grandson, and his daughter treats him much as she used to treat her doll.

In drawing such a character James is at the farthest remove from Balzac, whose most brilliant moral studies are those of the transforming and corrupting power which wealth exercises upon its possessor. James was always ready to confess that he did not have the shadowiest notion of business; but by picking a character like Adam Verver he obligated himself to some knowledge of the type of men who were making the great American fortunes—if not Dreiser's knowledge in *The Financier* and *The Titan,* at least that which Edith Wharton could show in *The Custom of the Country.* Without such knowledge he laid himself wide open to the most serious charge that can be levelled against a great novelist, what Yvor Winters has instanced, in the case of *The Spoils of Poynton,* as the split between manners and morals, the lack of congruity between the environment which would have produced a character and the traits which the author has imputed to him. Mr. Verver's moral tone is far more like that of a benevolent Swedenborgian than it is like that of either John D. Rockefeller or Jay Gould.

If James failed to see how vulnerable he was in his portrait of Mr. Verver, it may have been because his attention was concentrated on something else. It was the rule of his later air-tight structures, a rule under which even Edith Wharton finally grew restive, that every detail was to be subordinated to his main theme. And here that theme was again composed around his heroine. Through her, as through Milly Theale, he wanted to give his last quintessential expression to a quality which had long haunted him, not the intense yearning for life, but another phase of the American character as he had known it, its baffled and baffling innocence in contrast with the experience of Europeans. That again is a minor-keyed and feminine quality, more convincing in a daughter than in a father. But when Mrs. Assingham goes to the length of saying that Maggie 'wasn't born to know evil, she must never know it,' we are back in the world of Hawthorne, of Hilda and her doves in *The Marble Faun*. The flinching from experience on the part of Hawthorne's blonde girls was what D. H. Lawrence found the most repellent of American traits; and it must be added that James intended Maggie's 'goodness' which Colonel Assingham finds 'awfully quaint,' to have its own initiation into evil.

But quaint or not, James believed in the moral fineness and sweetness of the old-time simpler America, and believed, too, that even if Mr. Verver was a billionaire, he could still be colored by those qualities. From the point of view of Charlotte's sophistication, the continued intimacy between Maggie and her father is an astonishing 'make-believe': 'They were fairly at times, the dear things, like children playing at paying visits, playing at "Mr. Thompson and Mrs. Fane," each hoping that the other would really stay to tea.' But the core of James' intention in this relationship remains what it had been when he was first thinking of making a short story on the theme and had declared in his notebook: 'The *subject* is really the pathetic simplicity and good faith of the father and daughter in their abandonment.'

Such a relationship raises some interesting questions about James' grasp of psychology. He had altered several details which had fitted his original plan for a short piece, especially the simultaneity of the double marriage, and the precipitation of the situation by the daughter's French husband finding himself more attracted by his father-in-law's young wife. James made the Prince's adultery less reprehensible by having him break with his past in all honesty, only to find it catch up with him unexpectedly through Maggie's eagerness to have her father marry Charlotte. But James held to the important contributing factor, the reason why the lovers were thrown together so often, as he had first outlined it: 'A necessary basis . . . must have been an intense and exceptional degree of attachment between the father and daughter—he peculiarly paternal, she passionately filial.'

James wrote with a knowledge of the sophisticated society of his day. He had led up to his notebook entry with some general reflections on the international marriage, and how its 'queer crudity' offered 'plenty of opportunity for satiric fiction.' Observing, too, in the era that had united Lord Randolph Churchill with Jennie Jerome of Rochester, N. Y., that it was always the European man who married the American girl, 'never the other way round,' he then went on to contrast the American girl with the American man. He had been impressed with what E. L. Godkin had said to him about the growing cleavage between the two: the one 'with her comparative leisure, culture, grace, social instincts, artistic ambitions'; the other 'immersed in the ferocity of business with no time for any but the most sordid interests, purely commercial, professional, democratic and political.' One questions whether Godkin had used the word 'democratic' in just that sequence, though Henry Adams might have. James' conclusion about the relation of the sexes was also like that of Adams: 'This divorce is rapidly becoming a gulf—an abyss of inequality, the like of which has never before been seen under the sun.'

But James did not satirize the international marriage in *The Golden Bowl*.

No more did he develop that cleavage between the sexes. Instead he distributed what he had noted as the feminine traits between Maggie and her father. Another limitation that would be even more puzzling to the modern psychologist is the view James took of their relationship. Though Charlotte may protest that her husband treats her 'as of less importance to him than some other woman,' James regards this intimacy between father and daughter as 'perfectly natural,' exceptionally close, to be sure, and naively innocent, but without a trace of the pathological fixation that our novelists would now see in it. James occupies a curious border line between the older psychologists like Hawthorne or George Eliot, whose concerns were primarily religious and ethical, and the post-Freudians. When, in *The Bostonians,* he wanted to make a study of Olive Chancellor's violent possessiveness over Verena Tarrant, he could do it out of his knowledge 'of those friendships between women which are so common in New England.' But though he could understand Lesbianism without having to give it a name, just as he could understand the corruption of the children in *The Turn of the Screw,* he was elsewhere oblivious to sexual distortions which would seem an almost inevitable concomitant of the situations he posits. Take, for instance, *The Pupil,* where, in contrast with Mann's *Death in Venice,* there is no basis in homosexual attraction, and a consequent vagueness, as the story is handled, in accounting for why the tutor's attachment to his charge is so strong as to make him destroy his prospects on the boy's account. What it comes down to, again and again, is that James' characters tend to live, as has often been objected, merely off the tops of their minds. This is what caused a representative modern psychologist like Gide to conclude that James, 'in himself, is not interesting; he is only intelligent.' And what bothers Gide most in James' characters is the excessive functioning of their analytical powers, whereas 'all the weight of the flesh is absent, and all the shaggy, tangled undergrowth, all the wild darkness . . . ' But in works as different as *The Turn of the Screw* and *The Wings of the Dove,* James showed an extraordinary command of his own kind of darkness, not the darkness of passion, but the darkness of moral evil.

As far as *The Golden Bowl* is concerned, James was again bent on conjuring up a world of magical enchantment. If we want to understand his aims, we had better follow the first rule of criticism and turn to what he has done rather than to what he hasn't. Instead of belaboring further his social and psychological limitations, it is more revelatory to examine the positive values which he found in such a world. As usual we arrive at those values through a series of diverse registers. To a casual glance Fanny Assingham may seem the typical spokesman for James' milieu. It is she who enunciates the proposition upon which his narratives seem most to depend, that 'the forms . . . are two-thirds of conduct.' It is she who asks, 'What is morality but high intelligence?' It is she who seems most supplied with supercharged Jamesian adjectives. It is she, indeed, who pronounces Charlotte no less than 'sublime' for coming back from America to see her old school friend through her marriage with the Prince—though it remains for Charlotte and the Prince themselves to reach the ultimate transvaluation of ordinary meanings when they pronounce as nothing less than 'sacred' their obligation to conceal their adultery from the trusting Ververs.

Fanny is the champion player of that favorite Jamesian game of scrutinizing the motives of her friends. She has all the leisure necessary to develop her skill. Indeed, she says, at the time of the Prince's marriage, that she will give her life 'for the next year or two, if necessary' to finding a husband for Charlotte. Many readers have objected to her relentless overinterpretation of the least detail as being typical of what is worst in James. But a point generally overlooked is that James has provided her with a husband who is himself the staunchest anti-Jacobite on record. In the first of their interminable conversations, Fanny starts wondering why Charlotte has come back, only to have the Colonel answer, 'What's the good of asking yourself if you know you don't know?' That sets the tone for all his rejoinders. When Fanny goes on worrying, 'How will it do, how will it do?' he puffs his cigar: 'It will do, I daresay, without your wringing your hands over it.' He also undercuts her adjectives. At her description of 'astonishing little Maggie,' " 'Is Maggie then astonishing too?'' . . . he gloomed out of the window.' And when Fanny, undeterred, still pursues her flight and declares that she is beginning to make Maggie out as even 'rather extraordinary,' " 'You certainly will if you can," the Colonel resignedly remarked.'

The cynical Colonel is certainly not the author's spokesman, but he is a valuable facet of humor amid the too frequent solemnities of James' later style. What, however, should be just as clear is that Fanny's words are not to be treated as gospel either. She is perfectly willing to lie, and her sharp but barren lucidity is sufficient token that in James' scale of values there is a higher morality than that of 'high intelligence.'

What that morality consists in, James means to express through the final basis on which Maggie and the Prince are re-united. He views Amerigo sympathetically throughout. He makes him insist to Fanny on his 'good faith'; and almost his first words to Maggie are an assurance that he doesn't 'lie nor dissemble nor deceive.' In trying to comprehend his father-in-law, the Prince hits upon a formula that he might almost have found in *The Theory of the Leisure Class.* He figures that he is 'allying himself to science, for what was science but the absence of prejudice backed by the presence of money?' The life that the Ververs expect him to lead would also corroborate Veblen, whose book James had probably not read, though Howells had recognized its great importance in a review. The Prince is the extreme case of the man who is expected to be rather than to do, a shining exhibit of conspicuous waste. Colonel Assingham is right in asserting that the reason why Amerigo is tempted into his affair with Charlotte is that he has nothing whatever to occupy him. But the emptiness of his existence is even greater than James was aware. In concentrating so excessively on the personal relations of his quadrangle, he imagined for the Prince no further role than that of arranging his rare books and balloting once at his club. His height of 'sacrifice' is giving up on one occasion the opportunity of dressing for dinner.

Despite the evidence of such details, James was not satirizing either the

Prince or the Ververs. For he was capable of finding enough positive content in his heroine's drama to absorb him wholly, and to let him assert, just as he was finishing the book, that it was the best he had 'ever done.' Its dynamics are provided entirely by Maggie, who combines Milly Theale's capacity for devotion with Kate Croy's strength of will. James' values of the heart, in contrast to those of the mere intelligence, are realized in her to the full. She thus provides us with material for understanding his conception both of love and of religion. How much she embraces under the former, James attests in the passage where he has her declare to Fanny: ' "I can bear anything . . . For love."

> Fanny hesitated. "Of your father?"
> "For love," Maggie repeated.
> It kept her friend watching. "Of your husband?"
> "For love," Maggie said again.'

James means to convey thus the rare inclusiveness of her generosity; but the reader's mind is likely to be crossed also by a less pleasant aspect, by something slightly sickening in this wide-open declaration of being in love with love, without discrimination between kinds.

Yet Maggie is clear enough about what she wants when she sets out to win back her husband. The great scene, which James intensifies by framing in a way comparable to Strether's recognition on the river, is that in the fifth book, wherein Maggie perceives all the implications of what she is trying to salvage. The frame is provided by a great lighted window of the card-room in which the others are playing bridge, while Maggie paces up and down the terrace, looking in at them. Such a projection enables James to condense in a single visual image all the essential aspects of his drama: 'The facts of the situation were upright for her round the green cloth and the silver flambeaux; the fact of her father's wife's lover facing his mistress; the fact of her father sitting all unsounded and unblinking, between them; the fact of Charlotte keeping it up, keeping up everything, across the table, with her husband beside her; the fact of Fanny Assingham, wonderful creature, placed opposite to the three and knowing more about each, probably, when one came to think, than either of them knew of either.'

This is the perfect image for the Jamesian game. And the key to his kind of inner drama lies in Maggie's consciousness that though merely an absent observer, she is 'presumably more present to the attention of each than the next card to be played.' Breathless suspense is created by her sudden awareness that she might smash this harmony like the stroke of doom. The images here are extremely violent. Her temptation to cry out in denunciation assaults her, 'as a beast might have leaped at her throat.' She knows horror for the first time, 'the horror of finding evil seated all at its ease, where she had only dreamed of good; the horror of the thing hideously *behind,* behind so much trusted, so much pretended, nobleness, cleverness, tenderness.' But as she moves through the storm-charged night to the end of the terrace and around the house, she faces her alternatives with re-conquered control. The lighted empty drawing-room strikes her 'like a stage again awaiting a drama . . . a scene she might people, by the press of her spring, either with serenities and dignities and decencies, or with terrors and shambles and ruins, things as ugly as those formless fragments of her golden bowl she was trying so hard to pick up.'

The violence is never externalized. If Maggie is finally to have the golden bowl 'as it was to have been,' the decorum of appearances must be kept. She must defeat Charlotte without disturbing the peace, especially that of her father. But the scenes between Maggie and Charlotte are as charged with the energy of the unspoken as any that James ever wrote. As Maggie watches Charlotte leave the card-table, she has the sensation that a caged beast has escaped and is coming after her. But in the final conflict between them, the aggressiveness is all Maggie's. James makes her American self-reliance the equivalent of a religion. She is explicitly a Catholic, as her mother had been, but in her time of crisis, in contrast with Hawthorne's Hilda, she finds that she has no need of the Church. James' brief picture of Father Mitchell, 'good hungry holy man,' prattling and twiddling his thumbs over his satisfied stomach, is devastating, but he seems not to have intended any general satire of Catholicism, for which he elsewhere expressed respect as a conserving institution. His point is not that the Church has failed Maggie, but that her love and her own will are enough.

In contrast with Strether and Milly, and, indeed, with Newman, with Daisy Miller, with Isabel Archer, and with most of James' other Americans in Europe, the Ververs are not faced with defeat or renunciation, but with the consequences of complete triumph. The difference in James' ability to portray such values is considerable. He was aware of the danger of making Maggie overweening in her victory; and so she allows Charlotte to preserve her pride by having the last word, and by making it appear as though she herself had chosen to take Mr. Verver back to America. In addition, Maggie feels the pathos in Charlotte's situation. In one extraordinary passage when Charlotte is showing some visitors the art-treasures of the house, she becomes a tortured lecturer on herself as she recites her lesson: 'The largest of the three pieces has the rare peculiarity that the garlands looped round it, which as you see are the finest possible *vieux Saxe,* aren't of the same origin or period, or even, wonderful as they are, of a taste quite so perfect.' Unlike the Ververs, Charlotte, who has been brought up in Europe, is 'of a corrupt generation.' Yet as Maggie hears her go on, ' . . . its value as a specimen is I believe almost inestimable,' she is surprised that her own eyes are filled with tears. The quaver in Charlotte's voice is 'like the shriek of a soul in pain,' and the unspoken question with which Maggie looks across the room to her father is, 'Can't she be stopped? Hasn't she done it *enough?'*

Exactly what Mr. Verver thinks and feels about the situation is never given to us directly, since no word about it is allowed to pass between daughter and father. But James is clearly proud of Mr. Verver's share in the success. He notes once that this collector applies 'the same measure of value to such different pieces of property as old Persian carpets . . . and new human acquisitions,' but he never probes the implications of that anomaly. In a less special world, such a warping of fundamental values would have caused Mr. Verver to be portrayed as a Midas whose touch finally turned gold to horror. But Mr. Verver is happy to win back his rightful possession of his wife, and to take her along with his other museum-pieces as a benefaction to American City. His participation in the final action is symbolized by one of James' most strangely ambiguous images. The 'little meditative man' is described as 'weaving his own spell,' and presently that magic takes the form of an invisible silken halter or lasso around Charlotte's neck, to every twitch of which she must respond. This image is repeated on three occasions, and what James seems to want to keep uppermost through it is the unobtrusive smoothness of his 'dear man's' dealings. But James' neglect of the cruelty in such a cord, silken though it be, is nothing short of obscene.

James' failure to examine the premises of Mr. Verver's power led Ferner Nuhn to the ingenious conjecture of what this novel would have been like if recorded from Charlotte's point of view. He concluded that even 'the lovely Princess of the fairy tale' might then have turned out instead 'to be the bad witch.' James' treatment of Maggie, however, unlike his treatment of her father, is not incoherent. She has had her initiation into evil. She has won not only the Prince's respect for her forebearance, but also his deep love. As a result of what she has passed through, she can meet him now on the level of his mature wisdom: 'Everything's terrible, cara—in the heart of man.' And yet, through the very balanced manipulation of his denouement, James has shown the limitation with which Mark Ambient, one of his author-narrators, charged himself. He has 'arranged things too much . . . smoothed them down and rounded them off and tucked them in—done everything to them that life doesn't do.' In consequence, we can hardly escape feeling that Maggie, once more like Hilda, both has her cake and eats it too. She seems to get an unnatural knowledge of evil since she keeps her innocence intact.

Or perhaps the unsatisfactory nature of the positive values in this novel may be better described through the contrast between victory and defeat. In both *The Ambassadors* and *The Wings of the Dove* we are moved most deeply by loss and suffering. But there is an intrusion of complacence when Maggie, imaged repeatedly as a dancing girl, is said to be having 'the time of her life' in her sustained act. One reason why James was less convincing in imagining success was that he was unable to conceive it in any heroic form. In this he was a sensitive register of a time when American success was so crassly materialistic that, as we have noted, nearly all the enduring writers from that time voiced their opposition. But here, in his detachment, James was trying to invest his triumphant Americans with qualities they could hardly possess.

Or we may put it technically, that he did not find the 'objective correlative' for his theme. In every case we have seen that James' values went deep into his own past, even when he translated them into so different a milieu as Milly Theale's was from Minny Temple's. But when such innocent affection, such close paternal and filial relationships as characterized the James' family, are projected into a realm so unlike the one into which James had been born, we have reached the breaking point of credibility. Love is not enough to redeem a world like Maggie Verver's, as we can tell by a single glance ahead at the inevitably futile existence that any such Prince and Princess must continue to lead. A contrast with *The Scarlet Letter* recalls that the adultery there brought out a festering growth of hypocrisy and pride and vengefulness through which Hester Prynne had to struggle alone towards her redemption. And even if Hawthorne's narrative, like James', concentrated upon the personal relations of a very few characters, Hawthorne gave, through the depth of his moral perception, a sense of the larger society of which his characters were part. The inadequacy of *The Golden Bowl* in this respect makes it finally a decadent book, in the strict sense in which decadence was defined by Orage, as 'the substitution of the part for the whole.'

James himself suggested the weakness of this book when putting his finger on that of *The American*. In pointing out the lack of verisimilitude in having the Bellegardes relinquish the chance of getting Newman's money, he was led into a definition of romance which not only takes the discussion of Hawthorne's prefaces a step further, but also constitutes one of the major formulations about the nature of the nineteenth-century novel. James knew, from his own immersion in the development of that novel, that the separation, in the name of a self-conscious realism, between reality and romance, is false. He insists that 'the men of largest responding imagination before the human scene,' such as Balzac, commit themselves to both modes; that 'it would be impossible to have a more romantic temper than Flaubert's Madame Bovary, and yet nothing less resembles a romance than the record of her adventures.' But James does not blur the distinction: 'The real represents to my perception the things we cannot possibly *not* know, sooner or later, in one way or another . . . The romantic stands, on the other hand, for the things that, with all the facilities in the world, all the wealth and all the courage and all the wit and all the adventure, we never *can* directly know; the things that can reach us only through the beautiful circuit and subterfuge of our thought and our desire.'

We can tell from such a passage that, despite the conventional classification, James was very little of a realist. He held the test for the romance to be that whereas it deals with 'experience liberated,' with 'experience disengaged, disembroiled, disencumbered, exempt from the conditions that we usually know to attach to it,' it must not fail too patently to make its events correspond to our sense 'of the way things happen.' (Hawthorne, using the vocabulary of the mid-century, had said that the writer of romance may 'so manage his atmospherical medium' as to mellow the lights or enrich the shadows of his picture, but that he must not 'swerve aside from the truth of the human heart.') When James looked back to *The American*, after an interval of over thirty years, he believed that he had so failed. He was not to have our chance of seeing *The Golden Bowl* at that distance. But, whereas it now appears that *The Wings of the Dove* is his superlative example—perhaps the superlative example in our literature—of what can be liberated 'through the beautiful circuit and subterfuge' of thought and desire, *The Golden Bowl* forces upon our attention too many flagrant lapses in the way things happen both in the personal and in the wider social sphere. With all its magnificence, it is almost as hollow of real life as the chateaux that had risen along Fifth Avenue and that had also crowded out the old Newport world that James remembered.

From *Henry James, The Major Phase* (New York: Oxford Univ. Press, 1944), pp. 81-104.

LIONEL TRILLING

The Princess Casamassima

The Princess Casamassima belongs to a great line of novels which runs through the nineteenth century as, one might say, the very backbone of its fiction. These novels, which are defined as a group by the character and circumstance of their heroes, include Stendhal's *The Red and the Black,* Balzac's *Père Goriot* and *Lost Illusions,* Dickens' *Great Expectations,* Flaubert's *Sentimental Education;* only a very slight extension of the definition is needed to allow the inclusion of Tolstoi's *War and Peace* and Dostoevski's *The Idiot.*

The defining hero may be known as the Young Man from the Provinces. He need not come from the provinces in literal fact, his social class may constitute his simplicity and the high hopes he begins with—he starts with a great demand upon life and a great wonder about its complexity and promise. He may be of good family but he must be poor. He is intelligent, or at least aware, but not at all shrewd in worldly matters. He must have acquired a certain amount of education, should have learned something about life from books, although not the truth.

The hero of *The Princess Casamassima* conforms very exactly to type. The province from which Hyacinth Robinson comes is a city slum. "He sprang up at me out of the London pavement," says James in the preface to the novel in the New York Edition. In 1883, the first year of his long residence in England, James was in the habit of prowling the streets, and they yielded him the image "of some individual sensitive nature or fine mind, some small obscure creature whose education should have been almost wholly derived from them, capable of profiting by all the civilization, all the accumulation to which they testify, yet condemned to see things only from outside—in mere quickened consideration, mere wistfulness and envy and despair."

Thus equipped with poverty, pride, and intelligence, the Young Man from the Provinces stands outside life and seeks to enter. This modern hero is connected with the tales of the folk. Usually his motive is the legendary one of setting out to seek his fortune, which is what the folktale says when it means that the hero is seeking himself. He is really the third and youngest son of the woodcutter, the one to whom all our sympathies go, the gentle and misunderstood one, the bravest of all. He is likely to be in some doubt about his parentage; his father the woodcutter is not really his father. Our hero has, whether he says so or not, the common belief of children that there is some mystery about his birth; his real parents, if the truth were known, are of great and even royal estate. Julien Sorel of *The Red and the Black* is the third and youngest son of an actual woodcutter, but he is the spiritual son of Napoleon. In our day the hero of *The Great Gatsby* is not really the son of Mr. Gatz; he is said to have sprung "from his Platonic conception of himself," to, indeed, "the son of God." And James's Hyacinth Robinson, although fostered by a poor dressmaker and a shabby fiddler, has an English lord for his real father.

It is the fate of the Young Man to move from an obscure position into one of considerable eminence in Paris or London or St. Petersburg, to touch the life of the rulers of the earth. His situation is as chancy as that of any questing knight of medieval romance. He is confronted by situations whose meanings are dark to him, in which his choice seems always decisive. He understands everything to be a "test." Parsifal at the castle of the Fisher King is not more uncertain about the right thing to do than the Young Man from the Provinces picking his perilous way through the irrationalities of the society into which he has been transported. That the Young Man be introduced into great houses and involved with large affairs is essential to his story, which must not be confused with the cognate story of the Sensitive Young Man. The provincial hero must indeed be sensitive, and in proportion to the brassiness of the world; he may even be an artist; but it is not his part merely to be puzzled and hurt; he is not the hero of *The Way of All Flesh* or *Of Human Bondage* or *Mooncalf*. Unlike the merely sensitive hero, he is concerned to know how the political and social world are run and enjoyed; he wants a share of power and pleasure and in consequence he takes real risks, often of his life. The "swarming facts" that James tells us Hyacinth is to confront are "freedom and ease, knowledge and power, money, opportunity, and satiety."

The story of the Young Man from the Provinces is thus a strange one, for it has its roots both in legend and in the very heart of the modern actuality. From it we have learned most of what we know about modern society, about class and its strange rituals, about power and influence and about money, the hard fluent fact in which modern society has its being. Yet through the massed social fact there runs the thread of legendary romance, even of downright magic. We note, for example, that it seems necessary for the novelist to deal in transformation. Some great and powerful hand must reach down into the world of seemingly chanceless routine and pick up the hero and set him down in his complex and dangerous fate. Pip meets Magwitch on the marsh, a felon-godfather; Pierre Bezuhov unexpectedly inherits the fortune that permits this uncouth young man to make his tour of Russian society; powerful unseen forces play around the proud head of Julien Sorel to make possible his astonishing upward career; Rastignac, simply by being one of the boarders at the Maison Vauquer which also shelters the great Vautrin, moves to the very center of Parisian intrigue; James Gatz rows out to a millionaire's yacht, a boy in dungarees, and becomes Jay Gatsby, an Oxford man, a military hero.

Such transformations represent, with only slight exaggeration, the literal fact that was to be observed every day. From the late years of the eighteenth century through the early years of the twentieth, the social structure of the West was peculiarly fitted—one might say designed—for changes in fortune that were magical and romantic. The upper-class ethos was strong enough to make it remarkable that a young man should cross the borders, yet weak enough to permit the crossing in exceptional cases. A shiftless boy from Geneva, a starveling and a lackey, becomes the admiration of the French aristocracy and is permitted by Europe to manipulate its assumptions in every department of life: Jean Jacques Rousseau is the father of all the Young Men from the Provinces, including the one from Corsica.

The Young Man's story represents an actuality, yet we may be sure that James took special delight in its ineluctable legendary element. James was certainly the least primitive of artists, yet he was always aware of his connection with the primitive. He set great store by the illusion of probability and verisimilitude, but he knew that he dealt always with illusion; he was proud of the devices of his magic. Like any primitive storyteller, he wished to hold the reader against his will, to *enchant,* as we say. He loved what he called "the story as story"; he delighted to work, by means of the unusual, the extravagant, the melodramatic, and the supernatural, upon what he called "the blessed faculty of wonder"; and he understood primitive story to be the root of the modern novelist's art. F. O. Matthiessen speaks of the fairytale quality of *The Wings of the Dove;* so sophisticated a work as *The Ambassadors* can be read as one of those tales in which the hero finds that nothing is what it seems and that the only guide through the world must be the goodness of his heart.

Like any great artist of story, like Shakespeare or Balzac or Dickens or Dostoevski, James crowds probability rather closer than we nowadays like. It is not that he gives us unlikely events but that he sometimes thickens the number of interesting events beyond our ordinary expectation. If this, in James or in any storyteller, leads to a straining of our sense of verisimilitude, there is always the defense to be made that the special job of literature is, as Marianne Moore puts it, the creation of "imaginary gardens with real toads in them." The reader who detects that the garden is imaginary should not be led by his discovery to a wrong view of the reality of the toads. In settling questions of reality and truth in fiction, it must be remembered that, although the novel in certain of its forms resembles the accumulative and classificatory sciences, which are the sciences most people are most at home with, in certain other of its forms the novel approximates the sciences of experiment. And an experiment is very like an imaginary garden which is laid out for the express purpose of supporting a real toad of fact. The apparatus of the researcher's bench is not nature itself but an artificial and extravagant contrivance, much like a novelist's plot, which is devised to force or foster a fact into being. This seems to have been James's own view of the part that is played in his novels by what he calls "romance." He seems to have had an analogy with experiment very clearly in mind when he tells us that romance is "experience liberated, so to speak; experience disengaged, disembroiled, disencumbered, exempt from the conditions that usually attach to it." Again and again he speaks of the contrivance of a novel in ways which will make it seem like illegitimate flummery to the reader who is committed only to the premises of the naturalistic novel, but which the intelligent scientist will understand perfectly.

Certainly *The Princess Casamassima* would seem to need some such defense as this, for it takes us, we are likely to feel, very far along the road to romance, some will think to the very point of impossibility. It asks us to accept a poor young man whose birth is darkly secret, his father being a dissipated but authentic English lord, his mother a French courtesan-seamstress who murders the father; a beautiful American-Italian princess who descends in the social scale to help "the people"; a general mingling of the very poor with persons of exalted birth; and then a dim mysterious leader of revolution, never seen by the reader, the machinations of an underground group of conspirators, an oath taken to carry out an assassination at some unspecified future day, the day arriving, the hour of the killing set, the instructions and the pistol given.

Confronted by paraphernalia like this, even those who admire the book are likely to agree with Rebecca West when, in her exuberant little study of James, she tells us that it is "able" and "meticulous" but at the same time "distraught" and "wild," that the "loveliness" in it comes from a transmutation of its "perversities"; she speaks of it as a "mad dream" and teases its vast unlikelihood, finding it one of the big jokes in literature that it was James, who so prided himself on his lack of naïveté, who should have brought back to fiction the high implausibility of the old novels which relied for their effects on dark and stormy nights, Hindu servants, mysterious strangers, and bloody swords wiped on richly embroidered handkerchiefs.

Miss West was writing in 1916, when the English naturalistic novel, with its low view of possibility, was in full pride. Our notion of political possibility was still to be changed by a small group of quarrelsome conspiratorial intellectuals taking over the control of Russia. Even a loyal Fabian at that time could consider it one of the perversities of *The Princess Casamassima* that two of its lower-class characters should say of a third that he had the potentiality of becoming Prime Minister of England; today Paul Muniment sits in the Cabinet and is on the way to Downing Street. In the thirties the book was much admired by those who read it in the light of knowledge of our own radical movements; it then used to be said that although James had dreamed up an impossible revolutionary group he had nonetheless managed to derive from it some notable insights into the temper of radicalism; these admirers grasped the toad of fact and felt that it was all the more remarkably there because the garden is so patently imaginary.

Yet an understanding of James's use of "romance"—and there is "romance" in Hyacinth's story—must not preclude our understanding of the striking literal accuracy of *The Princess Casamassima*. James himself helped to throw us off the scent when in his preface to the novel he told us that he made no research into Hyacinth's subterranean politics. He justified this by saying that "the value I wished most to render and the effect I wished most to produce were precisely those of our not knowing, of society's not knowing, but only guessing and suspecting and trying to ignore, what 'goes on' irreconcilably, subversively, beneath the vast smug surface." And he concludes the preface with the most beautifully arrogant and truest thing a novelist ever said about his craft: "What it all came back to was, no doubt, something like *this* wisdom—that if you haven't, for fiction, the root of the matter in you, haven't the sense of life and the penetrating imagination, you are a fool in the very presence of the revealed and assured; but that if you *are* so armed, you are not really helpless, not without your resource, even before mysteries abysmal." If, to learn about the radical movement· of his time, James really did no more than consult his penetrating imagination—which no doubt was nourished like any other on conversation and the daily newspaper—then we must say that in no other novelist did the root of the matter go so deep and so wide. For the truth is that there is not a political event of *The Princess Casamassima,* not a detail of oath or mystery or danger, which is not confirmed by multitudinous records.

From *The Liberal Imagination* (New York: Doubleday, 1950), pp. 58-64.

ALLEN TATE

"The Beast in the Jungle"

JAMES'S "The Beast in the Jungle" was first published in a "volume of miscellanies" entitled *The Better Sort* in 1903. It was written at about the same time as Joyce's "The Dead," and although the fables of the two stories differ as profoundly as their techniques, they invite comparison at several levels. Both stories hinge upon climaxes of self-revelation, and both limit the reader's access to the subject to a central intelligence; both end with a powerful irony which we may call "classical irony" because its appearance has been predicted by the reader, whose interest is thus engaged at a higher level than that of mere surprise. We know that John Marcher and Gabriel Conroy are failing in some fundamental insight into their predicaments: our suspense looks ahead to the revelation of this failure to themselves. It comes, in both stories, in a short-view scene, toward which our interest has been directed in mounting intensity.

Again, as in "The Fall of the House of Usher" and "The Dead," we have the embodiment of the great contemporary subject: the isolation and the frustration of personality. It is a subject that goes back also to Poe's "William Wilson," and to Hawthorne in "The Bosom Serpent" and "Young Goodman Brown." Poe's method is nearer than Hawthorne's to the modern technique which grounds in psychological realism the symbolic representation of the hero's egoism. Hawthorne tends to scant the realistic base and to let his symbols become attenuated, into allegory. But it is a fact of curious and perhaps of important historical interest that Hawthorne was the first American writer (he may have anticipated anybody in Europe) who was conscious of the failure of modern man to realize his full capacity for moral growth. In four entries in *American Notes* he plays with this problem as the theme of a possible story, and he actually states the theme of "The Beast in the Jungle" some sixty years before the story was written:

> A young man and a girl meet together, each in search of a person to be known by some peculiar sign. They watch and wait a great while for that person to pass. At last special circumstance discloses that each is the one that the other is waiting for. Moral—that what we need for our happiness is often close at hand, if we knew but how to seek it.

To distinguish certain features of the method of "The Beast in the Jungle" we could scarcely do better than to use some of James's own critical terms. The "story" reduced to the slight action through which James develops the values of the situation, can be told very briefly. At a party John Marcher meets May Bartram; they renew a casual acquaintance of ten years before. Miss Bartram reminds him of a remarkable confession that he had made on that occasion: he had seen himself as a man to whom something overwhelming was destined to happen, and his part in life, excluding all other aims, was to await it— something special, even unique, for which he was to hold himself in readiness. He still feels the imminence of his destiny: it may come at any moment. Marcher and Miss Bartram now enter into a long, uncommitted relationship from which she gets nothing and he all that he can allow himself to get, since he must accept nothing short of his supreme moment. What he gets in the long run is her life, but he cannot "use" it since he can give nothing in return. They drift, in this moral stalemate, into middle age. Miss Bartram dies. Marcher feels increasingly empty and abandoned, and forms the habit of haunting her grave (one thinks here of the related story, "The Altar of the Dead"), until one day he looks into the eyes of another man haunting another grave. The man's eyes expose the depths of grief. The revelation forces Marcher into a tragic and ironic awareness. The supreme value for which he had reserved his life he had, of course, killed: it lay in the grave of May Bartram.

The story is laid out in six sections, and the point of view is consistently that of Marcher. The two first sections constitute a long foreground or "complication." It may be questioned whether the long complication is justified, since in it nothing "happens": in only about twice the space James lays the foreground of a very long novel, *The Ambassadors*. There are only two short-view scenes in the story. In slighting the scenic effect it is possible that James has violated one of his primary canons: the importance of rendition over statement. (There is too much of the elaborate voice of James, what Mr. Edmund Wilson has harshly described as the "Jamesian gas.") Yet one can see that he could not allow himself to get too deeply into Marcher's consciousness, at the stage of the complication, or Marcher himself would have had to examine his illusion too closely, and the story would have collapsed. The reader may well wonder whether the two brief scenic moments, when they finally come, are adequately prepared for, in spite of the length of preparation. James has not, in the first three sections, made either Marcher or Miss Bartram a *visible* character; he has merely presented their enveloping fate, as it *could* have been seen from Marcher's point of view; but we have seen them not quite credibly.

The excessive foreground is an instance of what James called the Indirect Approach to the objective situation through the trial-and-error of a Central Intelligence; but the Receptive Lucidity of a Strether, in *The Ambassadors,* is not at Marcher's command. Are we to conclude that the very nature of James's problem in "The Beast in the Jungle," the problem of dramatizing the insulated ego, of making active what in its essence is incapable of action, excluded the use of an active and searching intelligence in the main character?

The first of the two scenes appears in part IV when years of waiting have driven May Bartram to something like desperation. She cannot overtly break the frame of their intercourse, which permits her only to affirm and reaffirm her loyalty to the role of asking nothing for herself; in the act of a new reaffirmation,

"No, no!" she repeated. "I'm with you—don't you see—still." And as to make it more vivid to him she rose from her chair—a movement she seldom risked in these days—and showed herself, all draped and all soft, in her fairness and slimness. "I haven't forsaken you."

We return to Strether's mind, in which this reflection is all that the moment can give him:

. . . He couldn't pity her for that; he could only take her as she showed—as capable even yet of helping him. It was as if, at the same time, her light might at any instant go out; wherefore he must make the most of it. . . . "Tell me if I shall consciously suffer."

Here we get a special case of James's Operative Irony, which "implies and projects the possible other case." But the "possible other case" is not in the awareness of Marcher, as it always is in Strether; it is manipulated by James himself standing beside Marcher and moving May Bartram up close to imply her virtual offer of herself, her very body—an offer of which Marcher is not aware, so deeply concerned is he with his "problem." As May Bartram stands before him, "all soft," it is Marcher's Beast which has leaped at him from his jungle; and he doesn't know it.

It is a fine scene, unobtrusively arrived at, and it has a certain power. It is perhaps sounder in its structure than the second and climactic scene. Marcher's frequent visits to Miss Bartram's grave are occasions of a developing insight into his loss, his failure to see that his supreme experience had been there for him day after day through many years. But James must have known that, to make the insight dramatically credible, it must reach the reader through a scene; and to have a "scene" there must be at least two persons and an interchange between them. He thus suddenly introduces, at the last moment, what he called in the Prefaces a *ficelle*, a character not in the action but brought in to elicit some essential quality from the involved characters. The stranger haunting the other grave is such a *ficelle*; but not having been "planted" earlier and disguised, he appears with the force of a shock, and could better be described as a *deus ex machina*—a device for ending an action by means of a force outside it; here it serves to render scenically, for the eye and ear, what had otherwise been a reported insight of Marcher's. James could not let himself merely tell us that Marcher had at last seen his tragic flaw; he must contrive to show him seeing it.

If this story is the greatest of the James *nouvelles,* as it probably is, one must reconsider the generally held belief that it is his special form, in which he scored greater triumphs than he ever did in the novels. If we look at it in terms of the visible material—the material *made* visible—it is much too long; the foreground is too elaborate, and the structure suffers from the disproportion of the Misplaced Middle (James's phrase), that is, he has not been able to render dramatically parts I and II and "confer on the false quantity the brave appearance of the true." If the grief-stricken stranger at the end was to be more than a palpable trick, should not James have planted him (or his equivalent) somewhere in the foreground?

These questions do not exhaust the story, which remains one of the great stories in the language. In the long run its effect is that of tone, even of lyric meditation; and it is closer to the method of Hawthorne than one may at a glance suppose; for in the last scene it is very nearly allegory, though less so than that companion piece, James's great failure in spite of its own great tone, "The Altar of the Dead." In neither of these stories is the naturalistic detail distinct enough to give the situation reality; and the symbolism tends to allegory because there is not enough detail to support it. We must always turn to Joyce's "The Dead" for the great modern example of the *nouvelle*.

From "Three Commentaries," *The Sewanee Review,* 58 (1950), 5-10.

LEON EDEL

From *Henry James: The Untried Years*

THIS IS all Henry tells us of the "obscure hurt" and it is a queer tale—queer since he has mingled so many elements in it and at the same time thoroughly confused us about the time sequence. If the accident occurred at the "same dark hour" as the outbreak of the Civil War, that is in the "soft spring of '61" then the visit to the doctor "that summer" must have taken place during the summer of 1861. But "that summer" becomes, at the end of the account, the summer of 1862. The details, as given by Henry, are meagre; and they bristle with strange ambiguities: in his characteristically euphemistic manner he makes it sound at every turn as a matter grave and ominous while at the same time minimizing its gravity.

The hurt is "horrid" but it is also "obscure." It is a "catastrophe," but it is in the very same phrase only a "difficulty." It is a passage of history "most entirely personal" yet apparently not too personal to be broadcast to the world in his memoirs, even though when it happened he kept it a secret and regretted the necessity of making it known. It is also "extraordinarily intimate" and at the same time "awkwardly irrelevant." This is perplexing enough. James compounds the mystery by giving no hint of the kind of hurt he suffered, although at various times during his life he complained of an early back injury, which he usually dated as of 1862. That he should have chosen to omit all specific reference to his back in his memoirs is significant; in some way he seems to have felt that by vagueness and circumlocution he might becloud the whole question of his non-participation in the Civil War. To the error of omission—"error" because of the consequences of his reticence—must be added the effect of his elaborate euphemisms: the use of the words *intimate, odious, horrid, catastrophe, obscure* and the phrase *most entirely personal*. These had an effect not unlike that of the unspecified "horrors" of *The Turn of the Screw*. His readers were ready to imagine the worst.

What, after all, is the most *odious, horrid, intimate* thing that can happen to a man? However much different men might have different answers, in the case of Henry James critics tended to see a relationship between the accident and his celibacy, his apparent avoidance of involvements with women and the absence of overt sexuality in his work. Thus there emerged a "theory" promptly converted into a rumor that the novelist suffered a hurt, during those "twenty odious" minutes, which amounted to castration. In the April-June 1934 *Hound & Horn* issue, devoted entirely to Henry James, Glenway Wescott reported it almost as a fact: "Henry James, expatriation and castration. . . . Henry James

it is rumored, could not have had a child. But if he was as badly hurt in the
pre-Civil-War accident as that since he triumphed powerfully over other au-
thors of his epoch perhaps the injury was a help to him." Stephen Spender
quotes this passage in *The Destructive Element* and suggests that "Castration, or
the fear of castration, is supposed to preoccupy the mind with ideas of suicide
and death." He goes on to show how this is true of many of James's characters.
Mr. Spender, however, does have a second thought and adds in a footnote: "The
rumour of castration seems exaggerated and improbable, but it seems likely that
James sustained a serious injury." F. O. Matthiessen in *The James Family,*
speculates that "since Henry James never married, he may have been sexually
impotent . . . " R. P. Blackmur, in his essay in the *Literary History of the United
States* equates James with the emasculated Abelard "who, after his injury raised
the first chapel to the Holy Ghost"; so James, he adds, "made a sacred rage
of his art as the only spirit he could fully serve." And Lionel Trilling suggests
that "only a man as devoted to the truth of the emotions as Henry James was,
could have informed the world, despite his characteristic reticence, of an
accident so intimate as his." The obscure hurt remained obscure to these critics;
and to some of them highly ominous. . . .

Three days after the fire, on October 31, 1861, Perry's diary testifies to the
fact that Henry James was well enough to travel. "Thursday, Oct. 31 (1861)
At recitation in morning. Harry has gone to Boston." Perry by this entry
identified (for James's nephew) the visit to William that Henry mentions in
Notes of a Son and Brother. A letter from William to the family after Henry
returned to Newport speaks of the "radiance of H's visit." Had Henry suffered
anything approaching serious injury he would neither have been in condition
for journeying nor visiting; nor does it seem likely that William would have
found the visit "radiant." Henry remained for a long week-end. On November
5 Perry's diary says: "At school. Harry's before 12" and on the next day Henry
walked with his friend to Easton's Point.

The next few months are those to which Henry alluded when he spoke of
his seeking "to strike some sort of bargain" with his injury and his date of the
summer of 1862—apparently early summer—for the visit to the eminent surgeon fits. However limited medical knowledge may have been in that era, it
is quite clear that there would have been no "pooh-pooh" had the surgeon
discovered a groin injury or a hernia. Hernia operations had been performed
earlier in the century and any acute hurt would have been easily apparent to
an experienced medical man. The "obscure hurt" was obscure indeed. Some
years after the Newport fire Henry published a short story about a Civil War
veteran who survives the conflict without physical injury but is stricken by
illness at the end. The nature of the disorder is not disclosed; it is, however,
"deeply-seated and virulent." The attending physician tells the hero, whose
name is Colonel Mason, "You have opposed no resistance; you haven't cared
to get well." Mason tries and is aided by an affectionate aunt who takes him
to her home and gives him the care and attention of a mother. Staying with
her is a beautiful niece, Caroline Hoffman, with whom Mason falls in love;
he worships her, however, from afar; he gives her no intimation of his feelings.

When he discovers that Miss Hoffman has been wooed successfully by his own doctor he has a relapse. "It's the most extraordinary case I ever heard of," says the doctor as his patient dies. "The man was steadily getting well." And again: "I shall never be satisfied that he mightn't have recovered. It was a most extraordinary case." The story, entitled "A Most Extraordinary Case," appeared in the *Atlantic Monthly* of April 1868 when Henry was twenty-five.

The extraordinary case was as mystifying to the doctor as the obscure hurt was to Henry James. The doctor was, however, unaware of the subjective elements which caused Mason to give up the fight; and Henry James was unaware of the subjective elements which conditioned and at the same time obscured his hurt. He gives us a very positive clue in his final account when he asserts "what was interesting from the first was my not doubting in the least its (the obscure hurt's) duration." This is a curious and significant admission. James admits to foreknowledge or to a feeling that his injury would have lasting effects. We can, of course, explain this in part by saying that James was an extraordinarily intuitive person. Still, to know in advance that the hurt would have a "duration" is not intuition; it is an attempt at prophecy; it suggests in effect a wish that the hurt might endure, or at least betrays an extraordinarily pessimistic frame of mind about it. It was a pre-judgment which the doctor in Boston did not in any way endorse. To understand the real ground for James's certainty that he had a serious hurt that would prolong itself, we must reach back into the events of his father's life before he was born.

Fire had a special meaning in the life of the James family. A fire in a stable had an even more special meaning. The senior Henry's cork leg had been the symbol through all of Henry Junior's life of what could happen to someone who becomes involved in putting out a stable fire. It was an enduring injury. We can therefore speculate, and the evidence warrants it, that this is the explanation for Henry James's sense, from the moment that he had hurt himself in circumstances analogous to those of his father, that his hurt too would have a long duration. And this is what happened. Henry was still experiencing his back-ache late in life.

The theory that there was an unconscious identification with the father at the moment of the accident is reinforced by a similar identification which occurs in the account set down in old age. Describing his hurt as keeping "unnatural" company with "the question of what might still happen to everyone about me, to the country at large," Henry James said, as we have noted, that these "marked disparities" became "a single vast visitation." His use of these words evokes for us that other word which seems almost a portmanteau version of *vast* and *visitation.* . . . Henry James at the last could claim that he also had had his *vastation.* Two letters of William James's supply independent evidence as to the nature of Henry's ailment and fix it in his back. In a letter of 1867 William speaks of having "that delightful disease in my back, which has so long made Harry so interesting. It is evidently a family peculiarity. . . ." In the same vein, when Robertson James complained of a back-ache in 1869, William, by then a medical student, wrote "even if we suppose that this recent matter of your back is a false alarm, yet in virtue of the sole fact of your fraternity with Harry and me, you must have a latent tendency to it in you." . . .

In sum, the evidence points clearly to a back injury—a slipped disc, a sacroiliac or muscular strain—obscure but clearly painful. Perhaps the letter to Sturgis best describes it, "a strain subsequently . . . neglected." That the hurt was exacerbated by the tensions of the Civil War seems quite clear. Mentally prepared for some state of injury by his father's permanent hurt, and for a sense therefore of continuing physical inadequacy, Henry James found himself a prey to anxieties over the fact that he might be called a malingerer ("to have trumped up a lameness at such a juncture could be made to pass in no light for graceful") and had a feeling that he was deficient in the masculinity being displayed by others of his generation on the battlefield. This is reflected in all his early stories and contributed to the quite extraordinarily literal assumption by the critics that Henry James "castrated" himself in the accident. Of such substance are legends sometimes compounded. Yet even if we did not have the evidence of Henry James's activities immediately after the fire, his physically active life and his monumental production would in itself undermine the legend. An invalid could hardly have accomplished what Henry James did between the ages of twenty-one and seventy-three. He rode horseback, fenced, lifted weights (to fight off over-weight), took long daily walks and was an inveterate traveller, indulging in an expenditure of prodigious physical energy, over and above his fecundity in creation, which in itself is deservedly legendary; he spent hours daily at his desk; he combined literary labor with a crowded and intricate social life. There was nothing of the eunuch about him either in appearance or action. Henry James himself, we suspect, would not have used the word *eunuch* so freely, as he did on occasions, to describe bad and unproductive writers, had he been physically one himself.

From *Henry James: The Untried Years* (Philadelphia: J. B. Lippincott, 1953), pp. 175-76, 178-81, 183.

DOROTHY VAN GHENT

The Portrait of a Lady

THE TITLE, *The Portrait*, asks the eye to see. And the handling of the book is in terms of seeing. The informing and strengthening of the eye of the mind is the theme—the ultimate knowledge, the thing finally "seen," having only the contingent importance of stimulating a more subtle and various activity of perception. The dramatization is deliberately "scenic," moving in a series of recognition scenes that are slight and low-keyed at first, or blurred and erroneous, in proportion both to the innocence of the heroine and others' skill in refined disguises and obliquities; then, toward the end, proceeding in swift and vivid flashes. For in adopting as his compositional center the growth of a consciousness, James was able to use the bafflements and illusions of ignorance for his "complications," as he was able to use, more consistently than any other novelist, "recognitions" for his crises. Further, this action, moving through errors and illuminations of the inward eye, is set in a symbolic construct of things to be seen by the physical eye—paintings and sculptures, old coins and porcelain and lace and tapestries, most of all buildings: the aesthetic riches of Europe, pregnant with memory, with "histories within histories" of skills and motivations, temptations and suffering. The context of particulars offered to physical sight (and these may be settings, like English country houses or Roman ruins, or objects in the setting, like a porcelain cup or a piece of old lace draped on a mantel, or a person's face or a group of people—and the emphasis on the visual is most constant and notable not in these particulars, extensive as they are, but in the figurative language of the book, in metaphors using visual images as their vehicle) intensifies the meaning of "recognition" in those scenes where *sight* is *insight,* and provides a concrete embodiment of the ambiguities of "seeing."

In James's handling of the richly qualitative setting, it is characteristically significant that he suggests visual or scenic traits almost always in such a way that the emphasis is on *modulations of perception in the observer.* The "look" of things is a response of consciousness and varies with the observer; the "look" of things has thus the double duty of representing external stimuli, by indirection in their passage through consciousness, and of representing the observer himself. For instance, when Ralph takes Isabel through the picture gallery in the Touchett home, the "imperfect" but "genial" light of the bracketed lamps shows the pictures as "vague squares of rich colour," and the look of the pictures is Isabel's state at the moment—her eager and innately gifted sensibility and her almost complete ignorance, her conscious orientation toward an

unknown "rich" mode of being that is beautiful but indeterminate. Let us take
another example from late in the book. Directly after that conversation with
Madame Merle when Isabel learns, with the full force of evil revelation,
Madame Merle's part in her marriage, she goes out for a drive alone.

> She had long before this taken old Rome into her confidence, for in a world of ruins
> the ruin of her happiness seemed a less unnatural catastrophe. She rested her
> weariness upon things that had crumbled for centuries and yet still were upright;
> she dropped her secret sadness into the silence of lonely places, where its very modern
> quality detached itself and grew objective, so that as she sat in a sun-warmed angle
> on a winter's day, or stood in a mouldy church to which no one came, she could
> almost smile at it and think of its smallness. Small it was, in the large Roman record,
> and her haunting sense of the continuity of the human lot easily carried her from
> the less to the greater. She had become deeply, tenderly acquainted with Rome: it
> interfused and moderated her passion. But she had grown to think of it chiefly as
> the place where people had suffered. This was what came to her in the starved
> churches, where the marble columns, transferred from pagan ruins, seemed to offer
> her a companionship in endurance and the musty incense to be a compound of
> long-unanswered prayers.

Here the definition of visible setting—churches and marble columns and ruins,
and comprehending all these, Rome—though it is full, is vague and diffuse,
in the external sense of the "seen"; but in the sense that it is a setting evoked
by Isabel's own deepened consciousness, it is exactly and clearly focused. It is
Rome *felt,* felt as an immensity of human time, as a great human continuum
of sadness and loneliness and passion and aspiration and patience; and it has
this definition by virtue of Isabel's personal ordeal and her perception of its
meaning. The "vague squares of rich colour" have become determinate.

The theme of "seeing" (the theme of the developing consciousness) is fertile
with ironies and ambiguities that arise from the natural symbolism of the act
of seeing, upon which so vastly many of human responses and decisions are
dependent. The eye, as it registers surfaces, is an organ of aesthetic experience,
in the etymological sense of the word "aesthetic," which is a word deriving
from a Greek verb meaning "to perceive"—to perceive through the senses.
James provides his world with innumerable fine surfaces for this kind of
perception; it is a world endowed with the finest selective opportunities for
the act of "seeing," for aesthetic cultivation. But our biological dependence
upon the eye has made it a symbol of intellectual and moral and spiritual
perception, forms of perception which are—by the makers of dictionaries—
discriminated radically from aesthetic perception. Much of James's work is an
exploration of the profound identity of the aesthetic and the moral. (In this
he is at variance with the makers of dictionaries, but he has the companionship
of Socrates' teacher Diotima, as her teaching is represented by Plato in the
Symposium. Diotima taught that the way to spiritual good lay through the
hierarchies of the "beautiful," that is, through graduations from one form of
aesthetic experience to another.) Aesthetic experience proper, since it is acquired through the senses, is an experience of *feeling*. But so also moral

experience, when it is not sheerly nominal and ritualistic, is an experience of *feeling*. Neither one has reality—has psychological depth—unless it is "felt" (hence James's so frequent use of phrases such as "felt life" and "the very *taste* of life," phrases that insist on the feeling-base of complete and integrated living). Furthermore, both aesthetic and moral experience are nonutilitarian. The first distinction that aestheticians usually make, in defining the aesthetic, is its distinction from the useful; when the aesthetic is converted to utility, it becomes something else, its value designation is different—as when a beautiful bowl becomes valuable not for its beauty but for its capacity to hold soup. So also the moral, when it is converted to utility, becomes something else than the moral—becomes even immoral, a parody of or a blasphemy against the moral life (in our richest cultural heritage, both Hellenic and Christian, the moral life is symbolically associated with utter loss of utility goods and even with loss of physical life—as in the Gospel passage, "Leave all that thou hast and follow me," or as in the career of Socrates, or as in Sophocles' *Antigone*). Moral and aesthetic experience have then in common their foundation in feeling and their distinction from the useful. The identity that James explores is their identity in the most capacious and most integrated—the most "civilized"—consciousness, whose sense relationships (aesthetic relationships) with the external world of scenes and objects have the same quality and the same spiritual determination as its relationships with people (moral relationships). But his exploration of that ideal identity involves cognizance of failed integration, cognizance of the many varieties of one-sidedness or one-eyedness or blindness that go by the name of the moral or the aesthetic, and of the destructive potentialities of the human consciousness when it is one-sided either way. His ironies revolve on the ideal concept of a spacious integrity of feeling: feeling, ideally, is *one*—and there is ironic situation when feeling is split into the "moral" and the "aesthetic," each denying the other and each posing as *all*.

From *The English Novel: Form and Function* (New York: Holt, Rinehart and Winston, 1953), pp. 215-18.

R. P. BLACKMUR

The Loose and Baggy Monsters
of Henry James

MY POINT is that the technical or executive forms of Henry James, when turned into fetishes if not rules, have been largely misunderstood both with regard to themselves and with regard to their mutual relations with other forms. Both the ideal and the substantial origin of classic form has been ignored, on the one hand; and on the other hand, by critics concerned immediately with morals or what is called the liberal imagination, the poetic—the creative—aspects of James's language and the conventions of his forms have been minimized and cheapened to perception. I am not concerned to repair these damages but to meditate on them along several paths of meditation. The paths are well known and our feet fit them, if not our thoughts; we have only to fit our thoughts to the uneven ground.

One path is the parallel path of verse. In verse, we know that the meter does something to the words, even though the meter be the most rigidly prescribed arrangement of syllables. We know also that the rhythm does something to the meter and to the words, something not the same thing but related. Beyond that we know that the meter and rhythm and words do something to both the intellectual structure and the moral perception of the poem. We understand all this because we appreciate the strains separately as well as feel them together: we know that by their joint operation something has been brought into the poem, which is vital to it, and which would otherwise not be there. What we ought to know is that something comparable to this is true of the novel and we should suspect that we need training in appreciation to recognize it: training so that we may see not only what the author consciously intended but also where he struck on something over and above, or other than, what he intended. We must understand that the poetic mind is as much at work in prose as in verse, and we must understand that nobody—not even Dante, not even James Joyce—can be conscious of, or deliberately take care of, all the skills he uses in the moment of composition. The nine muses may be conscious, but they are too many to hear at once. The poor poet—the poor novelist—must be contented to hear what he can, yet must act with the pressure and power of the others in his writing fingers— the pressure and the power he can feel conscious of only as a haunt that has just left him.

No wonder then, if such is his case, he will confuse what he does know and can hear with what he does not know and cannot hear: a confusion sometimes made with great effect. Half the English poets of the seventeenth century thought that if technical mastery of the heroic couplet could be had, then the English epic might be written, when the fact was that the deep form—the underlying classic form—of *Paradise Lost,* not written in couplets at all, heroic or homely, had solved the problem of the epic for Milton: had solved the problem of what new phase of being the epic of Homer, Vergil, Dante had reached in Protestant, Christian, seventeenth-century England. Other powers, other skills of mind and sensibility had entered into the struggle than the poets knew; yet for all we know the argument over metrical form was the efficient agent for the birth of the new deep form. That there have been no Miltons since, counts nothing; there have been no Dantes since Dante; nor should we want any. It is only the path we want to follow.

If the argument about the heroic couplet helped produce Milton, and if the argument about the "very language of men" helped produce Wordsworth, and if the argument about the "heightened form of the best conversation of the time" helped produce Eliot and Yeats—all these along with a good many confusions and ignorances as to what else helped—then I think we might strike it rich for the field of the modern novel if we look at one of the most confused, most arrogant, and most fertile statements ever made—among so many—by Henry James. The statement is often quoted, and it comes in the Preface he wrote to the revised verson of *The Tragic Muse.* I suggest that it is there precisely because at the moment of writing James was prodded—his writing fingers were twisted—by the very muses of deep form that he was only hauntedly aware of. Since he was criticizing, not creating, his response was irritated.

The Tragic Muse, I may say, seems to me a failure as a Henry James novel precisely because its form is so nearly only executive form, and not, as James partly allowed, because he did not give the executive form warrant enough to remake the characters. I take this as the unconscious source of James's irritation in the following remarks.

> A picture without composition slights its most precious chance for beauty, and is moreover not composed at all unless the painter knows *how* that principle of health and safety, working as an absolutely premeditated art, has prevailed. There may in its absence be life, incontestably, as "The Newcomes" has life, as "Les Trois Mousquetaires," as Tolstoi's "Peace and War," have it; but what do such large loose baggy monsters, with their queer elements of the accidental and the arbitrary, artistically *mean?* We have heard it maintained, we will remember, that such things are "superior to art"; but we understand least of all what *that* may mean, and we look in vain for the artist, the divine explanatory genius, who will come to our aid and tell us. There is life and life, and as waste is only life sacrificed and thereby prevented from "counting," I delight in a deep-breathing economy of an organic form.

It is curious that James should have reversed the order of words in Tolstoy's *War and Peace,* and if we had time when we got done asking what the whole passage stands for we might ask what that reversal stood for. In brief I think it stood for not having read the book, if at all, with good will—for having read it with a kind of rudderless attention. The important thing is that *War and Peace* does have every quality James here prescribes: composition, premeditation, deep-breathing economy and organic form, but has them in a different relation to executive form than any James would accept. Indeed, put beside *War and Peace, The Ambassadors, The Wings of the Dove,* and *The Golden Bowl* are themselves "large loose baggy monsters" precisely because an excess use was made of James's particular development of executive form, and precisely because, too, of the consequent presence of James's own brand of the accidental and the arbitrary, and because these together make access difficult to James's own "deep-breathing economy and organic form." It is these last, however, that hold us to James as they hold us to Tolstoy, and it is in them that we must find the "principle of health and safety"—or of deep ill and final danger—which James found in consciously practiced executive form; just as we would have to show in Tolstoy that his practice was virtually tantamount to an admirable executive form, and must indeed have been so used by Tolstoy. In James we have to deepen the level of our interest in the creative process; in Tolstoy we have to show that the deep things of the mind and the sensibility must after all, when they become literature, be exercised as a game, in the delight of the mind's play, like water-lights, upon its experience. It is true that Tolstoy, in a worse case than Chaucer, denied any worth to his novels compared to life; and it is true that James insisted that literature stood for everything worth living in a free life: he was himself he said that obstinate finality, the artist. But we can afford the excesses of the great though we must counter with our own smaller excesses of inquiry to which the great were not committed. The "divine explanatory genius" will never appear to tell us why Tolstoy—let alone Dumas and Thackeray—is "superior to art," but it seems to me possible for a talent not divine at all to suggest why both Tolstoy and James made superior forms of art. Here our business is with James; and all we have to keep in mind of Tolstoy—of Cervantes, of Dostoevski, of Balzac and Flaubert, of Fielding, Smollett, and Scott—is that on the evidence of endurance and recurrence of interest, on the evidence of the always available and availing feeling of stature, such work must have in every significant sense at least its necessary share of "deep-breathing economy" and "organic form." We must assume that if we asked we might find out indications of how that principle worked and we can be certain that we could find in such work what James meant by the principle of composition which is what is here meant by executive form. The novel has changed, since Cervantes, and has taken on different aspects of the general burden of literature according to the phase of culture and the bent of the writer, but I doubt that since, with Cervantes, it first undertook a major expressive task, it has reached any greater degree of mastery or perfection or possible scope. It is only the criticism of the novel, not formerly needed, that has yet to reach mastery—a lack here sorely felt; and a lack you will feel for yourselves if you will think of the relatively much greater maturity of the criticism of poetry. To go on with the present job requires the assumption of a critical maturity we do not have in fact and which we do in fact need if we are to make full response to the novel.

From *The Lion and the Honeycomb* (New York: Harcourt Brace, 1955), pp. 269-73.

RICHARD CHASE

The Lesson of the Master

HENRY JAMES'S *Portrait of a Lady* (1880) was the first novel by an American that made, within the limits of its subject, full use of the novel form. By comparison, no previous American novel, even those of James, can claim to be fully "done." From James's point of view the older American romance-novelists had many faults. Some of these he singles out explicitly in his biography of Hawthorne, others, as was noted in Chapter I, he directly or indirectly deals with in his prefaces and critical writings. Cooper, Hawthorne, and Melville (actually James seems to know next to nothing of the last) relied too readily on extravagant events and startling characters. They failed to render experience fully. They failed to illustrate and dramatize connections and relations. They did not see (in the words of the Preface to *Roderick Hudson*) that for the true novelist "the continuity of things is the whole matter . . . of comedy and tragedy."

To read the first page of *The Portrait of a Lady* is to step into a world unfrequented by the earlier American novelists. A handsome pictorial representation, a fine old house, beautiful lawns and gardens, a group of people being set in motion—all these may be found in Cooper's *Satanstoe* or Hawthorne's *House of the Seven Gables*. But James's procedure is different from that of the earlier writers. The effect he seeks is more organic and self-contained. At the same time, there is more detail, more careful observation, for he has "researched" his subject—something which Hawthorne, as James said, tended to leave undone. We encounter at the very beginning the author's reference to his book as a "history" and we are perhaps reminded that in his essay "The Art of Fiction" (1884) he was to say that the novel should give the same impression of veracity as does history itself.

On the broad, sloping lawn of the mansion James calls Gardencourt we discover people taking tea, and they are finding it agreeable, not only because it tastes good but because drinking it is a mild ritual by which they show themselves to be a part of a way of life, a social order which we understand is to figure strongly in the book, as strongly as does the life of the Westchester aristocracy in *Satanstoe*. Yet the life of James's characters will be illustrated and dramatized with a far more exact and also a more poetic art than one can find in Cooper's novel.

To admit, as most readers would, that there is an element of poetry in *The Portrait of a Lady* is to admit that though it has all of the novelistic virtues, it has others too. There is a sense in which one might speak of the "poetry" of *Pride and Prejudice* or *Middlemarch*—a poetry of picture and scene, a poetry felt to belong to the organized effect of character, action, and setting. But this is, so to speak, novelistic poetry, of the kind every interesting novel has. *The Portrait* has it too, but it also has a further dimension of poetry, to understand which one must perceive that James's novel is akin to romance as the others are not.

It is an important fact about James's art that he gave up what he considered the claptrap of romance without giving up its mystery and beauty. Mr. Leavis in *The Great Tradition* is not interested in James as a romancer, but he nevertheless notes that James is a "poet-novelist" and says that he combines Jane Austen's skill of observing and dramatizing manners with Hawthorne's "profoundly moral and psychological . . . poetic art of fiction." This is very well put, and it supports the supposition of this chapter that a part of James's great program for improving the novel consisted of the reconstitution, on new grounds, of romance. Often one has difficulty in pinning down any one element of a James novel as belonging to romance because the author has so completely subdued and transmuted it to suit his exacting novelistic purposes. The element of romance becomes generally subverted and assimilated; yet in turn it imports the glow of poetry to the realistic substance of the novel. Which is to say in a different way what Mr. Leavis says in the following: "James's own constant and profound concern with spiritual facts expresses itself not only in what obviously demands to be called symbolism, but in the handling of character, episode, and dialogue, and in the totality of the plot, so that when he seems to offer a novel of manners, he gives us more than that and the 'poetry' is major."

The conscious assimilation of romance into the novelistic substance of *The Portrait* took place in two different ways. It was assimilated into the language of the book and produced a general enrichment of metaphor. It was also brought in in the character of Isabel Archer, the heroine, who is to a considerable extent our point of view as we read. Isabel tends to see things as a romancer does, whereas the author sees things with the firmer, more comprehensive, and more disillusioned vision of the novelist. Thus James brings the element of romance into the novel in such a way that he can both share in the romantic point of view of his heroine and separate himself from it by taking an objective view of it.

The metaphors of *The Portrait of a Lady* do not often rival the amazingly elaborate figures one encounters in James's later works, but by contrast with the usual practice of the novel at the time James wrote they are notably daring—so much so that sometimes they seem to lead a life of their own within the spacious world of the book, although in each case we are led to see the relevance of the metaphor to the course of events and to the pattern of unfolding significance. There is a paradox, says James in his Preface to *The Portrait,* in trying to write a fiction at once so complex and so ambitious. The paradox is that a novel so conceived must "positively . . . appear more true to its character in proportion as it strains, or tends to burst, with a latent extravagance, its mould." Metaphor offered to James a kind of repository or annex in which the latent extravagance of his imagination might take form. As has often been noticed the main figures of speech in James's novel—although the variety is rich—have to do with the house and the garden.

The metaphors are sometimes extravagant. For example we read of Isabel that "her imagination was by habit ridiculously active; when the door was not open it jumped out of the window." But that is a mere piece of fancy and reminds us less of the characteristic practice of James than of the quaint wit of Hawthorne. Ordinarily, James's metaphors, in *The Portrait* as elsewhere, are not quaint and concise. They are suggestively imaginative and they are likely to be given a tone of elevated levity which at once enjoys what is being said and takes note of its extravagance. As often as not the Jamesian metaphor shows that mixture of serious poetic imagination with humor which we find in other American writers, notably Melville, Mark Twain, and Faulkner. Although one would hardly mistake the style of any one of these writers for that of any other, all of them are fond of the serious, intricately sustained joke. Here is James speaking of Ralph Touchett's pose of facetious irony, which Isabel, in her earnest sincerity, finds baffling and also reprehensible. Sensing his inner despair and sorry that he is sickly, she wants to come directly to the "real" Ralph Touchett, but he himself explains the value of his pose:

> "I keep a band of music in my ante-room. It has orders to play without stopping; it renders me two excellent services. It keeps the sounds of the world from reaching the private apartments, and it makes the world think that dancing's going on within."
> It was dance music indeed that you usually heard when you came within earshot of Ralph's band; the liveliest waltzes seemed to float upon the air. Isabel often found herself irritated by this perpetual fiddling; she would have liked to pass

James finds the metaphor, once launched, too good to drop

> through the ante-room, as her cousin called it, and enter the private apartments. It mattered little that he had assured her they were a very dismal place; she would have been glad to undertake to sweep them and set them in order. It was but half-hospitality to let her remain outside.

The idea of leaving and entering a house, the contrast of different kinds of houses, the question of whether a house is a prison or the scene of liberation and fulfillment—these are the substance of the metaphors in *The Portrait of a Lady.* Figuratively speaking, the story told in the novel is of Isabel's leaving an American house—a way of life, that is—for a European house. Ostensibly she conceives of this as an escape from frustrating and cramping confinement to a fuller, freer, more resonant and significant life. Actually, it is not hard to see that although James has much admiration and tenderness of feeling for his heroine, he gives her an element of perverse Yankee idealism of the sort that he was shortly to portray in the more exacerbated form of positively *perverted* idealism in Olive Chancellor in *The Bostonians.* So that for all her dark-haired, gray-eyed beauty, her delightful young enthusiasm, and her zest for life, there is in Isabel a fatal susceptibility to a form of imprisonment worse than that she has escaped. Figuratively, the house in which she lives as the wife of Gilbert Osmond confines her in a hopeless imprisonment she could not consciously have imagined.

Isabel Archer may be said to have the imagination of romance most notably in the sense that she responds to character intensely only when it conceives of itself at a high level of abstraction and when its acts are symbolic of ideal values. When this imagination is confronted by an appealingly complex human being, such as Lord Warburton, it sees only "a collection of attributes and powers." Like the romancer, Isabel refuses to impute significance to human actions unless they are conceived as being exempt from the ordinary circumstances of life, whereas the genuine novelist sees in ordinary circumstances the inescapable root condition of significant actions.

So, to carry the analogy only one step along, James in the end brings Isabel's point of view around from that of the romancer to that of the novelist. Like *The Blithedale Romance, The Portrait of a Lady* explores the limits of romance. But whereas Hawthorne seems to admit that he cannot be the true novelist and thus surrenders the imagination of the novelist to that of the romancer, James does the opposite, affirming the primacy of the novelist's imagination. But though he rejects romance as a moral view of the world, he assimilates into the very substance of the novel, by means of metaphor and the charm of the heroine herself, the appeal of romance. Thus he is able to meet superabundantly the requirement for the novel which he calls in the Preface to *The American* satisfying "our general sense of the ways things happen" and at the same time he is able to provide the novel with the poetry of romance.

So much, and as it would seem, no more is to be done with *The Portrait of a Lady* as a romance. In James's books one catches hold of the romance only just as it is disappearing into the thicket of the novel. Thus it is a thankless task to pursue too long and arduously something that is always being assimilated into something else. James is not a romancer like Hawthorne or Melville; he is a novelist to the finger tips.

It is true that, compared with any English novelist one might mention, James shows a strikingly varied interest in the literary forms associated with romance. He is not interested in pastoral idyls, to be sure. But many of his novels, as Jacques Barzun has pointed out, have a strong element of melodrama, from the early *Washington Square* to the late *Wings of the Dove*. Yet none of his fictions end in the sheer horror produced by the unresolved tensions of melodrama. This is true, for example, of the late short novel *The Other House*. In the first two thirds of the book we have the conflict of a "good" woman and a "bad" woman, a tale of frustrated love and revenge, and the drowning by the bad woman of a little girl. But even this thriller runs afoul of Jamesian complications before we are through with it. It turns out that the villainous woman is not, after all, guilty of unalloyed villainy. It is shown that she has attractive qualities, and it is shown that although she committed a particularly repulsive murder, the moral question finally involves the conscious or unconscious complicity in the crime by several of the people around her. The conclusion of the book is rather feeble and unsatisfactory, but the crime is made to seem that of a social class and a particular way of life, a crime that is compounded by everyone's agreeing to hush it up. By this time the tale has become quasi-tragic and our minds are directed as in the plays of Ibsen, which influence *The Other House,* to a social problem, the corruption of the bourgeoisie. The abstract actions, the stirring contradictions, the relative freedom from social and moral perplexities that we look for in melodrama—all these are excitingly present in *The Other House,* but they do not see James through to the end. Instead he characteristically makes the attempt to assimilate the purely melodramatic elements of the story into a novelistic conception. *The Other House* is an instructive investigation, from the Jamesian point of view, of the limits of melodrama.

A more striking departure from the practice of the English novelists (for, after all, Dickens and Conrad, among others, make use of melodrama) is James's use of a symbolistic or allegorical poetry in the late novels—notably *The Wings of the Dove* and *The Golden Bowl.* That these novels are akin to poetry has long been recognized. For example, Stephen Spender once compared *The Golden Bowl* illuminatingly with Eliot's poems. And many people have noted a certain ritualistic poetry of sacrifice and elegy in *The Wings of the Dove* and have seen in this story of the betrayal and death of a blameless young woman a resemblance to Racine's *Iphigenia* and Shakespeare's *Othello.* And Quentin Anderson's argument that *The Ambassadors, The Wings of the Dove,* and *The Golden Bowl* constitute in their cumulative significance a "divine novel" allegorically presenting James's version of his father's Swedenborgian theology is an important discovery.

Nevertheless, it seems to me that the foregoing discussion of *The Portrait of a Lady* marks out in a general way the borders beyond which an examination of James's more poetic dimension cannot go without becoming irrelevant to the question of James as a master of the craft of the novel. Even in reading a book which has so beautiful a central conception as *The Wings of the Dove* one is not recompensed by the allegory for the vexation of finding a novel which is so attenuated and prolix. One reads it, that is, stubbornly *as a novel.* One sets out with high hope and is immediately gratified by the unsurpassable rendering, at the beginning, of Kate Croy and her incomparable father; one is impressed and interested by Mrs. Lowder and her household; one gives a slightly baffled assent to Merton Densher; one finds the diaphanous Milly Theale beautiful and touching. But then the *longueurs* set in, along with the infinitely syntactical language which seems to engross no recognizable experience, and we are forced to settle for two fine scenes: Milly confronting the Bronzino portrait at Lord Mark's country house and Densher standing in the rain outside the Venetian cafe recognizing through the window Lord Mark. In short the metaphorical effects of *The Wings of the Dove,* which contain a sort of half-rendered allegory, do not strike one, like those in *The Portrait of a Lady,* as forming a positively valuable component of the whole. They strike one, rather, as negative facts—attenuations of the naturalistic substance of the novel. It is not possible for James, given his characteristic genius, to render an allegory in the form of a novel. But it is possible for him to weaken a novel by giving it an elusive aura of allegory. This at least is what one feels in actually reading the book. The allegory assumes substance and significance when it is considered as a part of the history of ideas, but that is another matter.

From *The American Novel and Its Tradition* (London: G. Bell, 1958), pp. 117-22, 134-37.

HAROLD C. GODDARD

The Turn of the Screw

CONSIDER THE second governess for a moment and the situation in which she finds herself. She is a young woman, only twenty, the daughter of a country parson, who, from his daughter's one allusion to him in her story, is of a psychically unbalanced nature; he may, indeed, even have been insane. We are given a number of oblique glimpses into the young woman's home and early environment. They all point to its stifling narrowness. From the confinement of her provincial home this young and inexperienced woman comes up to London to answer an advertisement for a governess. That in itself constitutes a sufficient crisis in the life of one who, after one glimpse, we do not need to be told is an excessively nervous and emotional person. But to add to the intensity of the situation the young woman falls instantly and passionately in love with the man who has inserted the advertisement. She scarcely admits it even to herself, for in her heart she knows that her love is hopeless, the object of her affection being one socially out of her sphere, a gentleman who can never regard her as anything other than a governess. But even this is not all. In her overwrought condition, the unexplained death of the former governess, her predecessor, was enough to suggest some mysterious danger connected with the position offered, especially in view of the master's strange stipulation: that the incumbent should assume *all* responsibility even to the point of cutting off all communication with him—never writing, never reporting. Something extraordinary, she was convinced, lurked in the background. She would never have accepted the place if it had not been for her newborn passion: she could not bring herself to disappoint him when he seemed to beg compliance of her as a favor—to say nothing of severing her only link with the man who had so powerfully attracted her.

So she goes down to Bly, this slip of a girl, and finds herself no longer a poor parson's daughter but, quite literally, the head of a considerable country establishment. As if to import the last ingredient to the witch's broth of her emotions, she is carried away almost to the point of ecstasy by the beauty of the two children, Miles and Flora, who have been confided to her care. All this could supply the material for a nervous breakdown in a girl of no worldly experience and of unstable psychical background. At any rate she instantly becomes the victim of insomnia. The very first night she fancies that she hears a light footstep outside her door and in the far distance the cry of a child. And more serious symptoms soon appear.

But before considering these, think what would be bound to happen even to a more normal mentality in such a situation. When a young person, especially a young woman, falls in love and circumstances forbid the normal growth and confession of the passion, the emotion, dammed up, overflows in a psychical experience, a daydream, or internal drama which the mind creates in lieu of the thwarted realization in the objective world. In romantic natures this takes the form of imagined deeds of extraordinary heroism or self-sacrifice done in behalf of the beloved object. The governess' is precisely such a nature and the fact that she knows her love is futile intensifies the tendency. Her whole being tingles with the craving to perform some act of unexampled courage. To carry out her duties as governess is not enough. They are too humdrum. If only the house would take fire by night, and both the children be in peril! Or if one of them would fall into the water! But no such crudely melodramatic opportunities occur. What does occur is something far more indefinite, far more provocative to the imaginative than to the active faculties: the boy, Miles, is dismissed from school for no assigned or assignable reason. Once more, the hint of something evil and extraordinary behind the scenes! It is just the touch of objectivity needed to set off the subconsciousness of the governess into an orgy of myth-making. Another woman of a more practical and common sense turn would have made inquiries, would have followed the thing up, would have been insistent. But it is precisely complication and not explanation that this woman wants—though of course she does not know it. The vague feeling of fear with which the place is invested for her is fertile soil for imaginative invention and an inadvertent hint about Peter Quint dropped by the housekeeper, Mrs. Grose, is just the seed that that soil requires. There is no more significant bit of dialogue in the story. Yet the reader, unless he is alert, is likely to pass it by unmarked. The governess and the housekeeper are exchanging confidences. The former asks:

"What was the lady who was here before?"
"The last governess? She was also young and pretty—almost as young and almost as pretty, Miss, even as you."
"Ah then I hope her youth and her beauty helped her!" I recollect throwing off. "He seems to like us young and pretty!"
"Oh he *did,*" Mrs. Grose assented: "it was the way he liked everyone!"
She had no sooner spoken indeed than she caught herself up. "I mean that's *his* way—the master's."
I was struck. "But of whom did you speak first?"
She looked blank, but she coloured. "Why, of *him.*"
"Of the master?"
"Of who else?"
There was so obviously no one else that the next moment I had lost my impression of her having accidentally said more than she meant.

The consciousness of the governess may have lost its impression, but we do not need to be students of psychology to know that that inveterate playwright and stage manager, the subconscious, would never permit so valuable a hint to go unutilized.

Mrs. Grose, as her coloring shows and as the governess discerns, is thinking of some one other than the master. Of what man would she naturally think, on the mention of Miss Jessel, if not of Miss Jessel's running mate and partner in evil, Peter Quint? It is a momentary slip, but it is none the less fatal. It supplies the one character missing in the heroic drama that the governess' repressed desire is bent on staging: namely, the villain. The hero of that drama is behind the scenes: the master in Harley Street. The heroine, of course, is the governess herself. The villain, as we said, is this unknown man who "liked them young and pretty." The first complication in the plot is the mysterious dismissal of the boy from school, suggestive of some dim power of evil shadowing the child. The plot itself remains to be worked out, but it will inevitably turn on some act of heroism or self-sacrifice—both by preference— on the part of the heroine for the benefit of the hero and to the discomfiture of the villain. It is a foregone conclusion too, that the villain will be in some way connected with the boy's predicament at school. (That he really was is a coincidence.) All this is not conjecture. It is elemental human psychology.

Such is the material and plan upon which the dreaming consciousness of the governess sets to work. But how dream when one is the victim of insomnia. Daydream, then? But ordinary daydreams are not enough for the passionate nature of the governess. So she proceeds to act her drama out, quite after the fashion of a highly imaginative child at play. And the first scene of her dramatic creation is compressed into the few moments when she sees the stranger on the tower of Bly by twilight.

Whence does that apparition come? *Out of the governess's unconfessed love and unformulated fear.* It is clearly her love that first evokes him, for, as she tells us, she was thinking, as she strolled about the grounds that afternoon, how charming it would be suddenly to meet "some one," to have "some one" appear at the turn of a path and stand before her and smile and approve, when suddenly, with the face she longed to see still vividly present to her mind, she stopped short. "What arrested me on the spot," she says, " and with a shock much greater than any vision had allowed for was the sense that my imagina- tion had, in a flash, turned real. He did stand there! but high up, beyond the lawn and at the very top of the tower. . . . " Instantly, however, she perceives her mistake. It is not he. In her heart she knows it cannot be. But if her love is too good to be true, her fears, unfortunately, are only too true. And forthwith those fears seize and transform this creation of her imagination. "It produced in me," the governess declares, "this figure, in the clear twilight, I remember, two distinct gasps of emotion, which were, sharply, the shock of my first and that of my second surprise. My second was a violent perception of the mistake of my first: the man who met my eyes was not the person I had precipitately supposed. There came to me thus a bewilderment of vision of which, after these years, there is no living view that I can hope to give." What has happened? The hint that the housekeeper dropped of an unnamed man in the neighbor- hood has done its work. Around that hint the imagination of the governess precipitates the specter who is to dominate the rest of the tale. And because he is an object of dread he is no sooner evoked than he becomes the raw material of heroism. It only remains to link him with the children and the "play" will be under way with a rush.

This linking takes place on the Sunday afternoon when the governess, just as she is about to go out to church, becomes suddenly aware of a man gazing in at the dining room window. Instantly there comes over her, as she puts it, the "shock of a certitude that it was not for me he had come. He had come for someone else." "The flash of this knowledge," she continues, "—for it was knowledge in the midst of dread—produced in me the most extraordinary effect, starting, as I stood there, a sudden vibration of duty and courage." The governess feels her sudden vibration of duty and courage as the effect of the apparition, but it would be closer to the truth to call it its cause. Why has the stranger come for the children rather than for her? Because she must not merely be brave; she must be brave for someone's sake. The hero must be brought into the drama. She must save the beings whom he has commissioned her to protect. And that she may have the opportunity to save them they must be menaced: they must have enemies. That is the creative logic of her hallucination.

From "A Pre-Freudian Reading of *The Turn of the Screw*," *Nineteenth Century Fiction*, 12 (June 1957), 6-11.

SELECTED BIBLIOGRAPHY

The Works of Henry James

A definitive edition of James is not yet available. James revised many of his novels after their serial publication and before their first appearance in volume form. The novelist further edited and revised the novels for the twenty-six volume New York Edition, 1907-09. The text of this edition was reprinted, with additions, and edited by Percy Lubbock in 1921-23 in thirty-five volumes. For a list of James' major works, see the Table of Important Dates.

The Complete Plays of Henry James (1949) edited by Leon Edel is definitive. The dramatic criticism was collected by Allan Wade in *The Scenic Art, Notes on Acting and Drama, 1872-1901* (1948). The largest collection of manuscripts is in the Harvard library.

Letters and Biography

Dupee, F. W. *Henry James.* New York: Sloane, 1951.

Edel, Leon. *Henry James: The Conquest of London: 1870-1881.* Philadelphia: Lippincott, 1962.

Edel, Leon. *Henry James: The Middle Years: 1882-1895.* Philadelphia: Lippincott, 1962.

Edel, Leon. *Henry James: The Treacherous Years: 1895-1901.* Philadelphia: Lippincott, 1969.

Edel, Leon, ed. *The Selected Letters of Henry James.* New York: Doubleday, 1955.

Edel, Leon and Ray, Gordon N. *Henry James and H. G. Wells: A Record of Their Friendship, Their Debate on the Art of Fiction, and Their Quarrel.* Urbana: Univ. of Illinois Press, 1958.

Pelham, Edgar. *Henry James, Man and Author.* New York: Houghton Mifflin, 1927.

Lubbock, Percy, ed. *The Letters of Henry James.* 2 vols. New York: Charles Scribner's Sons, 1920.

Matthiessen, F. O. and Murdock, K. B., eds. *The Notebooks of Henry James.* New York: Oxford Univ. Press, 1947.

Smith, Janet Adam, ed. *Henry James and Robert Louis Stevenson: A Record of Friendship and Criticism.* London: R. Hart-Davis, 1948. A collection of letters.

Critical Studies

Barzun, Jacques. "Henry James, Melodramatist." *The Question of Henry James,* ed. F. W. Dupee. New York: Holt, 1945.

Beach, J. W. *The Method of Henry James.* New Haven: Yale Univ. Press, 1917.

Kahv, Philip. "The Heiress of All the Ages." *Image and Idea.* New York: New Directions, 1949.

Kelley, Cornelia P. *The Early Development of Henry James.* Urbana: Univ. of Illinois Press, 1930.

Leavis, F. R. *The Great Tradition.* New York: G. W. Stewart, 1948.

Liddell, Robert. "The 'Hallucination Theory' of *The Turn of the Screw.*" *A Treatise on the Novel.* London: Jonathan Cape, 1947.

Pattee, F. L. *The Development of the American Short Story.* New York: Harper, 1923. Calls James a "scientific realist."